SIGNPOST

FOR COUNTRY

LIVING

**Turning an Urban Dream into a Rural Reality…
….not a Nightmare.**

By Suzanne Ruthven & Garrett Kelly

Published by The Good Life Press Ltd. 2010

ISBN 978 1 90487 1811
A catalogue record for this book is available from
the British Library.

Published by
The Good Life Press Ltd.
The Old Pigsties
Clifton Fields
Lytham Road
Preston
PR4 0XG

www.goodlifepress.co.uk
www.homefarmer.co.uk

Set by The Good Life Press Ltd.
Cover designed by Rachel Gledhill
Printed and bound in Great Britain
by Cromwell Press Group

INTRODUCTION

Nearly everyone, at some point in his or her life, considers the prospect of moving to the country. This might stem from a childhood holiday memory of blue summer skies and buttercup-filled meadows. Or we feel urban pressures might be lessened if the pace of life was slower. We may even have decided to start a home-based business and that the economics of the venture could be better financed by downsizing to a rural property. Or the escalating crime on the streets and in the schools could persuade us that the children would benefit from living out of town.

Signposts for Country Living is a step-by-step guide to finding your dream home, settling down, becoming part of the community and avoiding the pitfalls often experienced by the 'incomer.' Putting in a little bit of extra effort at the beginning could make the transition from 'townie' much more successful and far less painful. Blundering about and trusting to luck just won't help at all.

Both authors are country born and bred and, having moved around rural England, Wales and Ireland over the past thirty years, know a thing or two about integrating with local communities. Garrett Kelly, originally from Kent, is a well-known figure in field sports and author of Champagne & Slippers and Suzanne Ruthven, a native of the Buckinghamshire/Northamptonshire borders, is editor of the literary magazine The New Writer and an author with some twenty published titles to her credit including several on country-lore.

By taking the 'magazine approach' of an informal, inclusive style rather than a patronising catalogue of dos and don'ts, the authors also draw on the experiences of a wide variety of people to provide humour and anecdotes. Whatever the reasons for you picking up this book in the first place, this is where the idea of moving to the country passes from being an impossible or impractical dream to a considered reality.

Following the Signposts for Country Living can most certainly help turn your urban dream into a rural reality – not a nightmare.

Contents

Chapter Four: Integration Or Alienation?

Re-inventing yourself
Fools rush in
It's where you do your shopping that counts
Fund raising
Footpaths and bridle ways
Modernised or brutalised?
The grapevine
'Don't call us ...'
A little bit of mystery does no harm
Having a sense of humour helps

Chapter Five: Livestock & Locals

If it's got fur or feathers - it bites
The class(less) system
The village idiot
Making the right approach
Free range animals and children
Acquiring livestock
When to say 'no'
The fox and the hen house
This little piggy went to market
.....and a pony for the children

Chapter Six: The Social Scene

The pub
The church
The village hall
The school
The Women's Institute
The County Show
Cheap holidays & Bank Holiday weekends
Go on a treasure hunt
The car boot sales
Farmers' markets

Chapter Ten: Country Reality

Define your new priorities
Reality v. illusion
Legislation
Financial considerations
'We couldn't live anywhere else'
When age begins to tell
A richer life
When dreams turn to ashes
Back to town

A few final words of caution

THe COUNTRY DReaM

Every weekend newspaper supplements and magazines feature articles extolling the virtues of living in the country – but it's not always as simple as it sounds. Moving house is said to be one of the most traumatic 'life events' at the best of times, but very often re-locating to the country can also mean adjusting to an unexpected time-warp, complete with all its attendant culture-shocks.

As Alexandra quickly discovered when she and husband Lewis moved north to live on a smallholding in Northumberland. "I couldn't believe that the only conversations in the village pub were about sheep, shooting or the local mart. At first I thought it was a way of freezing us out until I realised that they didn't have anything to say to us. Things changed when we got our own sheep, Lewis joined a local shoot and I began a regular stint at the Farmers' Market. Now we have to make a conscious effort not to talk 'shop' when we have friends to visit."

Successfully transporting the family to the country isn't just a question of having more elbow room and a pony grazing out in the paddock. There's a lot more to consider because this will mean a whole new lifestyle for both adults and the children – not to mention the dog, who may also be in need of therapy by the time it's all over! What begins as an urban dream can quickly assume nightmare proportions if we get it wrong. So start by asking yourself.....

'What sort of country dweller am I going to be?'

This is perhaps the first and most important question we need to ask ourselves before setting off on one of those nerve-racking jaunts to find the perfect country property. Buy several current copies of each of the following magazines from any good newsagent and get the family to read them from cover to cover. This simple exercise can be carried out at home before any house-hunting excursions take place and should, hopefully, result in a frank discussion that involves the whole family. This means everyone being completely honest with themselves and each other in acknowledging the combined family's limitations and its grasp of country matters.

[i] **Country Illustrated** features the 'soil in the blood' type countryman who sees the countryside as an integral part of his life, livelihood and heritage. Part of the exercise is comparing this approach with your own, and will give you an idea of the indigenous species you will encounter in the depths of rural Britain.

[i] **Country Living** is a monthly glossy that bridges the interests of those who are in the throes of moving, or would like to move to the countryside. While it features people, conservation, wildlife, cookery, rural houses and gardens, and country businesses, it will rarely be found in a working farmhouse kitchen.

[i] **The Countryman** was founded in 1927 and has maintained a rather genteel and romantic approach to country matters. It has never really reflected a true picture as it has resolutely refused to feature any reference to country field sporting events, which are still very much an integral part of rural life.

[i] **Country Smallholding** gives practical advice on small-scale poultry and livestock keeping (including breeding), country crafts, gardening and cookery. The approach is aimed at those who wish to establish a living from what they produce or rear on the land in the foreseeable future.

[i] **Home Farmer** classes itself as 'more kitchen table than coffee table' and caters for those who are looking for a better quality of life, healthier food; and directing them towards a realistic solution to their lifestyle dreams with practical articles tailored towards the smaller acreage.

Each magazine represents the differing country attitudes that will be encountered the length and breadth of rural Britain, and gives a simple guide on how and where we see the family fitting into the scheme of things. It may cause us to stop and consider whether we really could settle down and be happy in an isolated farming community, or whether our needs will be best catered for on the edge of a small market or coastal town.

Getting away from it all.....

The glittering prospect of getting away from the close proximity of other people, and all the attendant hustle and bustle of town life, is probably the most appealing reason behind a proposed move to the Shires or the West Country, not to mention escape from the noise of traffic and local industry with its pollution and parking problems.

One recently married friend, a City stockbroker, has a pied-à-terre in Charterhouse Square which he uses Tuesday to Thursday, and goes home to his family and their farmhouse in Warwickshire the rest of the week. The reason for this arrangement is mainly due to the long hours he works and airport access for overseas trips, but also because the London flat can't accommodate his Dalmatian dog, Dizzy. In reality, he's a country boy who never managed to adapt to City life (even when offered a job in Paris), because he felt the quality of life was better in the rural Midlands. He is now considering giving up his highly lucrative 'day job' to start a landscape gardening business.

From our own point of view there may have been several conscious decisions..... that it was time to take advantage of plummeting house prices. Perhaps we, or a member of the family, may have fallen victim to inner-city crime, are concerned about over-stretched health services or the lack of discipline within the education system. The rural idyll may have been kindled by a monthly subscription to Country Living and a regular supply of Jilly Cooper novels – neither of which feature plunging naked into a slurry trench in mid-winter to rescue an idiot piglet who's just fallen in. Country Living and Cooper don't 'do' pig slurry.

Neither should the countryside be seen as a haven of perfect calm and silence, because a working farm can produce a veritable cacophony of sounds and smells that can certainly rival any industrial site. Sound carries a very long way over open farmland and any property within three miles (as the crow flies) of a farmyard will be adversely affected by the noise from sheep, cattle and perhaps especially cockerels. Similarly, farmers begin work at 'sparrow-fart' and the monotonous throb of a generator powering the milking sheds is not a recipe for inducing sleep - especially if one of us intends commuting. In the summer months there will also be the sound of wagons rumbling through the village well into the night if the race is on to beat the weather and get the hay, silage, straw or grain under cover.

Whatever the reason for our proposed change of lifestyle, we should keep the move in perspective and not look upon it with the preconceived idea of an idyllic landscape of rolling hills, peaceful woods, rippling streams and sunny skies. Although the family may discover that a larger house gives everyone more privacy, country living will, sooner or later, throw up its own set of idiosyncrasies. As the man said: Be prepared!

Changing your lifestyle.....

Try to anticipate what changes the move may bring about in the pattern of the family's daily routine, both immediately and in the long term. Before making a definite choice about where we want to live, we should take into account the differences in the cost of living between one part of the country and another. For example, the higher cost of living in the South and the Home Counties compared with that on the other side of that mythical divide that begins and ends at Watford Gap - although this does appear to be levelling out. Also consider any climatic differences if thinking of moving from south to north; it can affect the growing season and may necessitate the acquisition of a polytunnel!

Generally speaking, rural living is far less competitive and materialistic than being in the town where, more often than not, we are judged by what we do and what we own. Different sorts of clothes and footwear are worn in the country and most folk tend to shop at the local branch of 'country store' rather than swanning around in designer labels. Country roads, pub car parks and gravel drives can cut the Jimmy Choos to ribbons! This is the land of shabby chic, and a battered 4x4 blends in better than the latest model Lexus – unless we're in Newmarket. Even the choice of vehicle is important. As the country question goes: "What's the difference between a hedgehog and a Range Rover?" "On a hedgehog all the pricks are on the outside."

If the family's social life is currently reliant on adult education classes, theatre, cinema, extensive sports facilities, etc., the prospect of standing on a muddy touchline for a village football match, or a concert in the Scout hall, might be a bit of a come down. One of the complaints from businesses, particularly restaurants opening up in rural areas, is that "local people aren't interested in spending money and without the incomers, businesses would go broke." Should we consider moving to a popular tourist area? There will never be a shortage of facilities and places to eat, but we still might have to book during the summer months.

Often the biggest demands will be put on the children, especially if they have been used to taking full advantage of the urban facilities. Initially they may find little in common with children from farming communities, although younger ones will fare better than older siblings who are just finding their way into designer clothes, i-pods and stuff. This is another reason to question the wisdom of isolating the family from the society of like-minded souls, when a property on the edge of a small market town might solve any problems before they happen. Just consider that every time they want to go somewhere, either you or your partner will have to turn out on a cold winter's evening and drive miles to both deliver and fetch them.

On the plus-side, as Paula found out, her children are invited for more 'stop-overs' with friends from school. She discovered that these are arranged in a much more informal way than in the town. "This is more often than not a casual arrangement made at the school gates, and we come home minus a chick, or with one belonging to some other mother hen. In town any suggestion like that would have been treated with the gravest suspicion."

The dog, of course, will find his own set of social problems to contend with but, dogs being dogs, he'll soon be happily paddling through slurry and bringing home a decomposing roadkill.....

Working from home.....

There is a certain luxury in the prospect of working from home, but it can also be counter-productive if we have problems in disciplining ourselves to set working hours. "That first year I produced next to nothing," said Barbara, who moved to Monmouth from the Midlands. "I was supposed to be providing the illustrations for a children's book but I kept stopping to watch all sorts of birds I'd never seen before. When the lambs came, I couldn't stop watching them either. It wasn't until the publisher threatened to pull the plug on the commission that I forced myself back to work."

Being more positive about the extra time on our hands means that it is possible to make an early morning start and be finished by lunchtime; or even to work far into the night if a job needs to be finished. Linked to 'civilisation' by e-mail, mobile and fax, Philip found that he'd more time to spend with the family. "I had to get up at 5 o'clock every morning to commute to work before we moved, so getting up at six and just having to go downstairs to the study was sheer luxury. I'd already done half a day's work by the time my secretary was in the town office, had breakfast with the children before they went off to school and walked the dog down to the shop to fetch the morning paper."

Others find that working from home isn't all that it's cracked up to be. Very quickly they miss the cut and thrust of a business or commercial environment, and even become desperate for the inane chatter of colleagues who had previously bored them to death. Couples working together from home can also find that that their conversation has shrunk to Lilliputian-sized sound-bites and, as a result, the telephone bills rise astronomically as long-distance calls provide a much needed lifeline to friends left behind in the town.

Self-sufficiency.....

The popular television series, The Good Life, still has a lot to answer for when it comes to the lure of self-sufficiency. For many, the dream of a vegetable plot brimming over with Nature's bounty is only a fork's throw away. They see themselves serving freshly picked vegetables, fruit and salad to weekend guests, the pantry stocked with home-made preserves and pickles and the freezer crammed with surplus produce to tide them through the winter (not to mention the new-laid eggs, home-reared lamb and goat's cheese.....)

"I was full of grand ideas for the garden and in my mind's eye saw rows and rows of lush vegetables," said Margaret from Wales. "In reality the soil is only about four to six inches deep on top of solid slate and my ambitious kitchen garden was reduced to the type of vegetables suitable for raised-bed gardening. I still manage a reasonable crop every year but it wasn't what I'd imagined, and I wish I'd taken more notice of the quality of the soil before buying the house."

If all we've ever done is grow mustard and cress in a saucer, or kept a few supermarket-bought herbs on the windowsill, then self-sufficiency could be rather an ambitious project until we've become acclimatised. Vegetable gardening is subject to its own natural laws and it might be a couple of years before we really get to grips with the soil.

Good soil will grow anything – with a bit of common sense; although the structure of the soil will govern what can be best grown on it. Pay careful attention to what the area's been used for, and take a garden fork with you to turn over a few feet of the proposed plot. Is it clay? Light loam? Heavy loam? Chalk? The worst case scenario is heavy clay. This is not good for vegetable growing and the only remedy is good (ie. expensive) drainage and manuring, in addition to knowing when to work the ground according to weather conditions.

If we intend rearing our own goats, sheep or pigs, then a pig will dig out anywhere that needs clearing. Put a pig in an overgrown field for a year and it will rout out all the rubbish, plus the manure will be useful for future vegetable production. Sheep, on the other hand, need good grazing, so there's no point sticking them in an overgrown paddock. They only graze on open, short, well-kept pastureland; apart from hill sheep who, by nature, have adapted to survive on mountainsides. Goats eat everything and anything, including vegetables, fruit trees and garden shrubs! They are highly destructive, brilliant escape artists and, to be honest, put very little back into the land. "Does their manure justify the destruction they do? I doubt it," said one farmer.

Obviously it pays to put as much consideration into viewing the garden and any land as we would normally put into choosing the house. After all, if one of our prime reasons for moving includes the acquisition of land for gardening and/or rearing livestock, then we need to know what might cause problems in the long-term.

For.....

Needless to say, there are always fors and againsts as regards moving into the rural heartland, but one thing that can't compare is the natural beauty of unspoilt countryside, with each county having its own distinctive landscape. The air is undeniably cleaner and the environment usually much more relaxed than in the town. Food is also much fresher and often much cheaper if bought from a local Farmers' Market.

Depending on the area, we can usually get more for our money in terms of property, although rural properties are currently holding their prices compared with the towns. Country properties often have much bigger gardens, with paddocks and natural features such as a stream and woodland. Insurance rates for both houses and cars tend to be lower and there are seldom problems with parking.

Local medical services may not be as convenient but this is usually compensated for by a more personal level of treatment from staff both in general practice and local hospitals. There's still a lot of old-fashioned courtesy to be found in country communities. The crime rate is still lower in rural areas too and violent crime is less endemic, although wherever we go these days the drug culture is ever present.

Discreet incomers rarely have any difficulty in being invited to join local activities, particularly if there are small children involved. Small towns often have surprisingly impressive arts programmes and the cost of a ticket is usually a fraction of the amount charged in the city. Plus well-behaved dogs are great ice-breakers, and are often welcome in the local pub.

Against.......

Rural areas can be very inhospitable in winter, especially if we are thinking of moving near the coast. Fog, high winds, the damp, penetrating cold and roads that are often not gritted or cleared of snow can make travel an uncertainty.

In more isolated areas the house may have no mains gas or drainage, which means relying on bottled gas and the vagaries of a septic tank

15

or cesspit. It may even be necessary to cart the weekly rubbish some distance to the nearest pick-up point.

Public transport may be next to non-existent with hospitals, sports facilities and schools miles away. If there is only one family car then shopping may be restricted to the village shop or garage, which can be expensive, although internet shopping with the larger supermarkets is now popular in rural areas for precisely this reason. Emergency services will take much longer to arrive because they usually have to cover a wider area.

Needless to say, getting on with the neighbours is a must, and so is the willingness to join in community activities if we want to be accepted. Our social life will always involve travelling some distance for the theatre and cinema, and in the more rural areas much of the social activity revolves around traditional country activities and sports.

Not forgetting too that the dog will be permanently damp and clogged up to his armpits in mud.....and will never ever learn to wipe his feet before jumping on the sofa.

Village or town?

Be aware of the fact that many smaller villages in remote areas are dying. Young local people cannot afford the house prices that have escalated way beyond their means, and so many of them have been forced to move away. The lack of young families means there is often now no need for the village school and, with diminishing amenities such as a general store and/or Post Office, the village becomes a 'dormitory' with hardly any signs of life during the day.

The choice of whether to choose a property in a small village needs to be weighed against the family's long term needs:

• Check out the distances for school runs and not just the immediate requirements but also well into the future, including further education.

• Look at local amenities catering for adolescents and teenagers. Will this create problems in the long-term?

• What about family hobbies and interests: are there any facilities within easy reach of where you want to live?

- Will some members of the family be totally reliant on other members to ferry them around?

Alli and Jim bought their remote cottage when their three children were at primary and junior school age. By the time they'd reached the tween-ages, the parents found themselves turning out twice nearly every night to take them to Brownies, youth club, the pony club, football or choir practice, because there was no public transport after six o'clock. The days of drinks in the evening were over, because they had to wait until all the children had been rounded up before they could sit down and relax with their customary gin 'n' tonic. Although a friend's parents would often collect or deliver one child, there were still the other two to cater for.

Small towns with a more regular access to public transport often give the best of both worlds. Check out the regional railways and see whether these offer a wider access for schooling or social activities. Although the initial plan might have been for a more isolated property, a similar type within walking or cycling distance of a small rural town might present a more acceptable compromise. Remember, unlit country lanes can be very spooky after dark.

.....or a weekend cottage?

Those who decide to buy a weekend cottage instead of moving lock, stock and barrel, can and do manage to integrate into the community because they make an effort while they are there. However, if the decision comes up in favour of a weekend retreat, don't automatically expect the local people to fall over themselves to be neighbourly since the weekend cottagers are often held responsible for the moribund state of many of the smaller villages.

Radical plans drawn up for controlling the numbers of weekend retreats on Exmoor and in Pembrokeshire could see a drastic change in the planning laws across the rest of Britain where local people are finding themselves priced out of the market by wealthier outsiders. Many rural communities welcome the ideas, blaming second home owners for the closure of local schools, shops and Post Offices as these properties stand empty for most of the year, contributing little to the local economy. Planners in the other National Parks in England and

Wales have been closely monitoring the implementation of these proposals while the District Council for the New Forest has even been looking at ways to prevent outsiders from buying or renting homes in the area. And at the most extreme end of the spectrum, don't forget the burning down of second homes by a small number of extremists in the 1970s.

"There are a lot of second homes in the villages near here and their owners contribute hardly anything," said one local. "They arrive with their car boots already stocked full of food, so they don't need to shop locally. Since one cottage was sold as a holiday home the owner has spent no more than three weeks here. The garden is overgrown and the place just stands empty. What good is that to anyone?"

The perfect weekenders are those who struggle through the Friday night traffic after a hard working week, but still manage to put something back into the community. By using local suppliers and putting in a regular appearance at week-end activities (such as the village fete, church coffee mornings and sporting events), they stand head and shoulders above those who only show their faces at the village shop when they've forgotten the milk, having bought all their other provisions from Sainsbury's before leaving town.

Cookery writer for The Daily Telegraph, Josceline Dimbleby, found the Friday night-Sunday night marathon had little appeal. She soon realised that although some people seemed to thrive on weekend cottage life, it wasn't for her. It simply wasn't enjoyable, and neither was it relaxing. As she worked from home, a compromise was made and the family settled for a real second home, to which she could decamp with the children for all the summer holidays, "... and an easy train ride for my husband when he could get away," she added.

The weekend cottage might seem like an ideal solution, but few people seem to keep it up for long. Sooner or later the enthusiasm wanes and the cottage goes back on the market. Far from being a haven of relaxation, the family gets fed up with the travelling, especially during the winter months. The dog, however, sulks from Monday morning until Friday evening until he can get back to his chums at the local hunt kennels.

Getting your priorities right.....

In other words, why do we want to move? If the answer is because we can afford a bigger house to impress visiting family and friends, then we might be blinded to the many disadvantages of acquiring a large, draughty farmhouse or old mill. It's a well-known fact that free-standing houses in exposed positions are costly to heat, and if the property is in the 'green belt' area, planning permission for extensions and alterations may be severely curtailed. An acre of garden may not sound much but it can quickly become a chore if none of the family members are keen gardeners.

Should we insist on moving from an inner-city flat or small terrace to a large house with an even larger garden, then consider the long term maintenance of the extra land. The larger (and older) the property, the greater the degree of personal responsibility, and so be prepared to devote a considerable amount of time to keeping the roof, gutters, fences, walls, plumbing and drains in good repair. There will be more maintenance and redecorating, especially if the house does stand in an exposed position.

Moving to a much bigger house also means that more furniture, furnishings and appliances will be needed – and the insurance may also be proportionally much higher. For a house or cottage with a thatched roof, the premiums may be as much as four times higher again, although it does pay to shop around. Even though the house may be isolated with few amenities close by, council tax and water charges may come as a bit of a surprise if you move to a much larger property, or come under the jurisdiction of a different local authority. One couple found that the annual council tax on a house they wanted to lease in a remote corner of Wales was in the same band as the one they were selling in a prestigious and amenity-laden area in the Midlands!

More important still, avoid making promises about acquiring any livestock until the family has fully settled in, otherwise within a week of getting the keys you'll be called upon to come up with the goods. If the children are running true to form there will be a shopping list for two ponies, a goat, a couple of cats, another dog, two Jacob sheep, a Vietnamese pot-bellied pig and half a dozen hens. Few people realise how costly animals are to keep, so wait until there's some expert advice to call upon before buying anything with fur or feathers.

None of this should deter anyone from pursuing a rural dream, but it is advisable to come to some sort of general agreement within the family before we start looking. It may also mean that it is advisable to reconsider certain priorities and available finances, especially in the current economic situation.

Highways and byways.....

One last word.... If we are considering a move to some really remote corner of Britain, check on the access by road, rail and air for the benefit of family and friends – especially if we have elderly relatives, and may need to get to them in a hurry. One couple found it took them nearly as long again to navigate the B-roads from the motorway turn-off to their home as it did to drive all the way from London. Also make enquiries about the cost of cheap-rate rail or air fares.

Despite all the British Rail jokes, it is often the easiest way to travel and, depending on the region, can be cheaper than taking the 4x4 if you book in advance. If you are considering buying a four-wheel drive vehicle, do explore the possibilities because 'Chelsea tractors' are not an unnecessary luxury in the country in wet weather – especially with a wet dog in tow!

FINDING A HOUSE

House hunting from a distance can be an extremely risky business, especially if we are unfamiliar with the area. It can also be quite a drain on the finances if it's a case of travelling back and forth to look at properties and there aren't any family or friends with whom we can stay. Jonie and Michael wasted a considerable amount of time and money flying all over the country in answer to advertisements that appeared in the property papers. Sometimes they travelled hundreds of miles only to find that the place was already under offer, or that the land was completely unsuitable for their requirements.

"No matter how closely we cross-examined the advertisers on the phone, it usually turned out that the 'desirable detached residence with paddock and outbuildings' was a derelict property in the fag-end of nowhere," said Michael. "It didn't matter that we'd explained that we needed something we could live in straight away; we drove all the way to Scotland, only to find the farmhouse had no windows and hadn't been occupied for five years."

A good place to start is by buying (or borrowing) a few current issues of Farmer's Weekly or Horse & Hound, which will give the names of estate agents specialising in country properties for sale or rent in the classified section. If you have a particular spot in mind, go into the reference library and go through Willing's Press Guide for details of the regional daily or weekly newspapers covering the area. There are also a number of 'relocation agencies' who, for a fee, act solely on behalf of the buyer to help find them the type of property they want. You could even contact Phil and Kirsty on 'Relocation, Relocation' if you felt lucky. And finally, invest in a large-scale 'trucker's' road atlas of Britain so that you can pinpoint exactly where the village is located.

The Properties Misdescriptions Act (1991) and the Trades Description Act has, in law, put restrictions on the more extravagant and misleading agents' particulars, but as we should remember from those long-forgotten Latin classes: caveat emptor, or 'let the buyer beware.'

Deciding on the right area.....

Needless to say, all sorts of personal, family and domestic issues will govern the choice of area of our new home, so we must try and resolve as many as possible if they are going to restrict our options. For example, those who fancy the idea of living in Wales should bear in mind that children will be required to learn y Cymraeg, as the Welsh language is known. Would this present a problem, especially with older offspring? Rather than hitting the British Isles like random elf-shot, begin by eliminating those locations which, for a variety of reasons, are no-go areas. Again, if one of the family's prime interests is sailing, then avoid the prospect of a 3-4 hour drive in holiday traffic each time a visit to the coast is planned, no matter how tempting the inland property might be.

Once an area (that is well within our price-range) has been decided upon, it will be in everyone's best interests to stay in 'bed & breakfast' for a few days in order to assess the 'feel' of the place. The advantage of using a B&B is that the proprietor will usually supply all the local gossip, especially if involved in the selection of estate agents and any likely properties. This is the sort of information not available for love nor money in a hotel and can save hours of trekking around town centres, libraries, council offices and tourist information bureaux..... and more valuable than any Home Information Pack! Make a thorough tour of the surrounding area and mark on the map the places you find particularly attractive.

If an extended visit to the area isn't possible, go onto the internet or have a chat with the agent who is selling your existing property and ask if they have any contacts, or whether they can give any information from the professional journals about agents that specialise in country properties. Some agents are linked to a regional network that can supply details of property in other areas, but you don't always get what you ask for. Don't get irritated when a selection of 'two-bed semis with off-road parking and no garden' are received, when the original specification clearly stated 'four beds plus 1 acre minimum!' The details or particulars may be presented in a variety of ways, from a list with only the briefest of information to a glossy brochure with colour photographs of the interiors, but do remember that any pictures may have been cropped to conceal less favourable sights.

Rosemary, a horticulturalist, went to view her dream country cottage that was listed as 'ideal for modernising' and discovered just four stone walls with a roof and constant running water - in the form of a stream that had diverted itself through the front door and out the back! "There was an interesting collection of rushes growing through the flagstones in the kitchen," she recalls.

It may be that when the time comes for serious looking, the type of property we were dreaming of is much too expensive in the original area we'd chosen. This, again, is where local knowledge comes in, because often the difference between affordable and unaffordable may simply be a variation in the post code, or a county border. Country properties with a small amount of land don't stay on the market for long, so we need to be quick off the mark and have our finances sorted out before we go looking. On the other hand, if the property has been hanging around for a long while, we need to know why.

"We sold our house in London, put the bulk of our furniture into store and took a holiday-let for the winter," said Annie. "That way we kept a roof over our heads while we got to know the area. We heard of a smallholding coming up for sale via the village pub. We went, we saw, we offered cash and the whole business was settled in less than a month and we already knew quite a lot of the local people because we'd lived in the village for four months. The added advantage was that we'd seen what the place was really like in winter!"

As Jonie and Michael found, one of the real problems of farmhouse hunting at a distance is that by the time the estate agent's list reached them, the only properties they were really keen on had already been snapped up. This is another reason why it's a good idea to take a few days and make personal contact with an agent in the area, because his (or her) knowledge of the local property market should be able to provide all the advice about the suitability of houses, locations and prices. If something interesting comes up, they may offer to phone or email instead of sending the details by post.

In many cases, the desire to move to a particular location has been a dream for years because so many holidays have been spent in the area, and it feels almost like home. But don't be tempted to move because friends live nearby. If the friendship doesn't come up to expectations, you could land up feeling even more isolated than ever if you haven't made attempts to widen your social circle. And some areas are notoriously insular by nature.

A recent newspaper report highlighted the plight of 'incomers' being treated as outcasts, having moved into the Fenland. "The fens have always been a bit insular," admitted a Kent farmer, whose family originally came from that area of Norfolk. "The locals are known as the Fenland Tigers because of their hostility to outsiders and they don't welcome the invasion of 'townies' who are seen as being responsible for the increase in house prices. "Similarly, a tongue-in-cheek response to a serious complaint in a rural newspaper claiming a 12-year residency in the area made the writer a 'local,' pointed out that his family had moved into the area in 1900, but were still considered 'blow-ins' by neighbours whose forebears were active in the area in the 1600s!

What kind of accommodation?

Of course, we all have lottery-fuelled dreams of moated, medieval manor houses, but realistically we usually settle for something only slightly larger than the house we've just sold. With either a parcel of land big enough to keep a couple of ponies; or with a generously sized traditional cottage garden.

We also have to accept the fact that unless we're very lucky, no single property is going to offer everything we want in a family home. This is where the whole family should sit down together and decide what the priorities are. Once agreement has been reached, make a checklist of all the essential features the new home must have, ie. number of bedrooms and reception rooms; study or family room; a Rayburn or Aga; a downstairs cloakroom etc., and any aspects that are non-negotiable. Despite the universal accolades for the Aga/Rayburn, a more functional cooker is also essential due to the unpredictable drain on the heat in the oven and hotplates – sprouts often taking three times longer to cook. This kind of cooking is an art form, so don't imagine you'll have it mastered in five minutes!

One prospective buyer refused to even consider any property with a downstairs bathroom. "I'd grown up in a cottage with a downstairs bathroom and it was an absolute nightmare," said Sue. "People thought I was mad because I wouldn't even look at a property with a downstairs extension, which certainly narrowed my choice when it came to country cottages, but since I knew I wouldn't be making an offer, I'd just be wasting everyone's time."

Have photocopies made of the checklist and take a fresh one for each viewing so you can make any necessary notes to provide a reminder of what took your fancy and clip it to the estate agent's particulars. There may, however, be one or two extra things that should be taken into account that may not be important when living in the town:

- There should be a reasonably sized entrance hall, porch or utility room that can easily accommodate coats, muddy Wellington boots, umbrellas and a wet dog.

- A downstairs lavatory is essential, otherwise everyone will be trailing in from the garden and all over the new carpets to go upstairs. One couple bought their cottage on the strength of the outside brick-built privy because they were both keen gardeners and thought it a highly civilised idea. The previous owner had used it for storing the dustbin.

- There should be adequate space for a reasonably sized freezer.

- Farmhouse kitchens tend to be the hub of the household, but do you want somewhere where members of the family and the dog can relax? Small breakfast rooms are ideal for converting into a television room, so the sitting room can be kept as a mud-free zone.

- Is there a particularly large piece of furniture that will need special consideration?

- Is one room needed for an office/study?

- Are outbuildings needed for any proposed hobbies/business use?

Surprisingly, a survey by a property website revealed that house hunters are more likely to put their pets' needs before those of the children. In fact, pets' needs rated only second after location by 41% of the poll. Beverly Cuddy, editor of Dogs Today, wasn't surprised by the result: "The family dog is increasingly considered when house hunting.....large, dog-proof gardens are high on the des-res list for a discerning doggie house buyer....."

"Once I'd decided on the location, the deciding factor was finding a suitable property for the dog," said Stewart. "It may not start out as a conscious decision, but one of the first things that goes through your mind when viewing is there's no room for the dog's bed, or the garden isn't secure, or is there anywhere to go for a walk?"

Obviously the priorities will vary from family to family, and an older couple without children living at home are not going to want the same things that are necessary for a young family. We don't like to think we're getting older, but if we're looking at buying a property once we've reached our fifties or sixties, we need to make sure there's adequate facilities should failing health mean we can't negotiate the stairs in ten years' time. Huge gardens may give a great deal of pleasure now, but will they become an insurmountable problem in later years?

Long distance family.....

Initially, some families go for the option of moving out of town with the children and dog, while the 'bread-winner' remains in town during the working week, travelling down on Friday night and returning to the metropolis early on Monday morning. There isn't quite the upheaval each week as there is with the weekend cottage, because the home front is permanently maintained - but it does bring its own share of difficulties.

If this is one of our options, we must check on how convenient the local services are for trains and bus routes. Will the remaining partner have use of a car? If not, is there easy access to a Post Office, bank, library, shops and health services? Is it easy to walk to a shop/Post Office and back carrying heavy shopping and/or manoeuvring a push-chair?

On a more personal level, is the 'weekend' partner going to feel resentful about the family integrating into the community without them? It may be that after braving commuter trains to get home to the family on Friday night, they may just want to sit down and relax.

Stephen, a lawyer, found he was becoming more and more irritated by the fact that as soon as he walked in the door, Chris would reel off a list of things that had been scheduled for the weekend. "If we weren't going into town, or to the cinema, we would be going out to dinner at someone's house. Chris was building up her social life, but these people were strangers to me. I just wanted to chill out and be at home since I was living in rented rooms during the week. Although I felt I was committing professional suicide, eventually I chucked in the town job and joined a local practice. I'm still not sure if I did the right thing."

Lloyd's circumstances were similar, although he was a born and bred city boy, while Lucy was a country girl. "Lucy's got her horses and dogs, but when we married I said right from the start that I would not bury myself in the country. I remain in town for most of the week and can go down whenever I choose. If either of us has an important social event to attend, then we put ourselves out to support each other, but most of the time we tend to lead separate lives. It wouldn't suit everyone, I suppose, but it works well for us, and the children are much better off living down there."

Conversely, Jackie was the career woman who didn't want to give it all up when she married John, who was a third generation farmer. "We met at a friend's wedding and so wouldn't have normally mixed in each other's circles. But we did, and we got married. I'm not cut out to be a farmer's wife. I've put in a lot of blood, sweat and tears to get where I am and I don't want to give it up. Am I being selfish? I don't think so. Anyway, we're trying for a family and that will mean me altering my lifestyle, so perhaps I'll be able to work from home and compromise."

If the long-distance family is an option, the important thing is to make sure that the new house is within easy reach of a motorway or train station. There's nothing more tiring than another hour's drive through dark, twisting country lanes on a miserable winter's night. The stay-at-home partner must also make allowances for a weary traveller who might not want to come home to an empty house – or a house full of people. This kind of lifestyle needs quite a lot of juggling, and is far from easy in terms of keeping everyone happy.

How to view.....

Make sure you've got a copy of your checklist clipped to the estate agent's particulars. It is important to try to visualise what the place will look like with your furniture in situ, and if you do have any large items to consider, make sure that you've got a tape measure to check on the actual size of the rooms since estate agent's particulars err on the side of generous, or often don't mention certain obstructions like air vents, alcoves, small windows, etc.

It's also a good idea to take a small compass and check the alignment of the house and garden so that you can tell which rooms benefit from maximum sunshine, and which will be affected by bad weather. A room that never gets any sun can be extremely unwelcoming in winter, so check your compass and find out which room faces where: a north facing room will be cold and dark, a south facing room will be warm and sunny for most of the day, an east facing room will get the morning sun and a west facing room will enjoy any glorious sunsets.

Some otherwise picturesque properties are located by a pretty stream in a wooded glen, but only ever see the sun at midsummer when it is directly overhead because the steep wooded hillsides block out any natural light. For the rest of the year the house remains in shadow, so gloomy and dark that lights have to remain on during the day. So take a compass and check the orientation of the building. This is important!

If you are viewing in winter.....

Take special note of the positions of any large trees and any over-looking properties. Again, by using a compass it is possible to work out whether the garden catches the sun all day or whether it is partially or even always shaded. Don't forget that leaves can make all the difference in summer too – a south facing sitting room can be extremely gloomy if there is a large tree in full leaf obstructing the sunlight. Try also to ascertain whether severe weather conditions could make access difficult, or if there is a stream or river close by that could cause flooding. Remember the floods of recent years have had an adverse effect on insurance cover, both inland and on the coast.

And don't think it's safe even if you're half way up a mountain, as Jim and Trish found out. "We're quite high up, but when there is heavy rain (which there always is in Wales) the land drains can't take all the water. Where the main road and lane converge outside our cottage, it runs like a river. Luckily we're on a high bank, but cottages lower down in the village often have flood water lapping over the doorsteps."

As far as any paddocks or pastureland are concerned, is there a supply of running water for livestock? The last thing we need is to be carting buckets of icy water in the depths of winter. Is the land well drained? Are there any boggy patches? Are the ditches dug out? Is the fencing sound enough to contain livestock? Are there thistles, nettles or ragwort? Is the pasture in good order or overrun with weeds? Even in winter there will be clear signs of neglect. Drainage, however, is the most important issue if you want to keep any form of livestock. Walk the boundaries and look at the ditches. "You don't want to see rushes growing unless there's a pond nearby," said a countryman.

If you are viewing in the summer.....

Take into account any neighbouring properties that may look straight into your family rooms when the leaves are gone. Also try to judge whether the new house will catch the neighbour's leaves in the autumn. "Our neighbour has two glorious sycamores, but every autumn it's our garden that is filled by the leaves because the wind blows them over the fence. You don't realise just how many leaves there are on a tree until you have to clear up someone else's," commented one new villager ruefully.

When viewing pastureland in summer, look for cracked soil as an indication of clay. If the land is bare of grass with lots of weeds, docks, nettles, thistles and ragwort, then it will be useless for livestock. On well-tended pastureland you won't see them, just good lush grass. "During hot summers the rubbish survives and the stuff you want to survive disappears," explained our tame countryman.

As we've already said, no house will meet your exact requirements, so take the following into consideration:

- Is the house what you really want?
- Does the layout suit your domestic requirements?
- Will there be enough room for how you want to live?
- Will your existing equipment/furniture fit?
- Is the location of the house right for the whole family?
- Is the property in good repair?
- Are there mains services: gas, electricity, water and sewerage?
- Will you be able to maintain/decorate the property yourself?
- Will you be able to manage the land/garden without help?
- Are there sufficient outbuildings?
- What's the condition of the drive, access road?
- Is there a secure area for the dog?

Take all these things into account, then go away with your check-list and talk it over. Score the aspects you have agreed are essential for your plans and lifestyle and compare scores with any competing propertes. Highlight any problem areas and deal with these first - but if you do decide that the property isn't right for the family, please have the courtesy to inform the vendor if you've promised to go back later in the day.

Check out any possible problem areas.....

Even if the house seems to suit all your requirements it is still important to go back to see it at different times of the day and if possible on a different day of the week and (time permitting) under different weather conditions. If it is a market town or a tourist area, make at least one visit on market day, or over the weekend, and check out the levels of traffic.

Sometimes peaceful country roads can become race tracks at certain times of the week. "The road outside the farm gates became a favourite run for bikers because there were no traffic restrictions on that particular stretch," said one incomer. "The perpetual scream of motorbikes made Sunday afternoons in summer an absolute misery." Heavy lorries may also use a particular road on weekdays, but not be in evidence at weekends.

Social activities in the countryside often mean there are a lot of vehicles parked on the verges and along narrow lanes. Another 'incomer' took exception to cars being parked outside his house by the Sunday morning congregation attending the village church. This had been going on for as long as anyone could remember without complaint, and no one ever blocked his driveway. Nevertheless, he got a bee in his bonnet and an almighty row ensued involving the parish council, the county council and the bishop. It broke the monotony of village life for months when he started leaving offensive personal notes on the windscreens of the church-goers' parked cars.

A property overlooking a farmyard may also bring about a different sort of invasion. If there are animals nearby then in the summer there will be flies, especially if the house is in close proximity to the muck-heap or any penned animals. Laura's home was a converted stable block with a kitchen window that opened onto a farm track. One evening she walked into the kitchen to find an extremely large Hereford bull with its head stuck through the window, eating the vegetables she'd left on the drainer for the family's supper.

Buying an old house....

Some people want the satisfaction of buying an old property to renovate it to their own design, and this can open up the options if it is the property rather than the land that is the attraction. Some local authorities are now refusing to grant planning permission for the conversion of barns to residential properties, but there are other options:

• disused churches or chapels
• railway or canal properties
• forestry workers' housing
• disused warehouses or mills
• redundant schoolhouses
• redundant pubs

If buying an old property to renovate, it may be that you will have to consider living in a caravan or a mobile home on the site for a long time. Planning permission and improvement grants can take up to 12 months, or even longer in Ireland! What may be a sunny hillside in mid-summer, however, can turn out to be very bleak in mid-winter, with the whole family, including a wet dog, crammed into a 20 foot caravan.

A word of warning: don't assume that planning permission will be granted. Under town and country planning laws, certain buildings are designated to be of special architectural or historical interest. A listed building may not be altered or extended in any way that alters its character or appearance. Certain places are designated conservation areas – sometimes this can be a whole town or village, or a square, a street, or even part of a street. The rules are strict and cover the whole of the buildings, inside and out, including outbuildings and boundary walls.

When the renovation work on Hilary's cottage revealed that the building was part of a medieval priory with Templar connections, a hysterical planning authority moved in and delayed the project for three years while the appropriate tiles and timber were found to complement the ancient roofing, stonework and staircase. And it's not only very old buildings that are listed. Some listed properties may only be 50 years old if they are of unusual design, or have some important local significance. The local authority search made by your solicitor will show whether the property is a listed building or is in a conservation area and any breach of the regulations is a criminal offence.

Some older properties have footpaths running across the land that can cause all sorts of difficulties, should you decide to apply to re-route them. One farmhouse has an old footpath that runs through the stable yard and when the owner's planning application to re-route it was halted due to the foot and mouth outbreak, he encountered all sorts of problems. Work on his approved extension went ahead, but the issue of re-routing the footpath was stopped and the delay meant that the application had to be re-advertised and, as a result, objections have now been raised over the proposed 35 yard detour.

Sounds and smells.....

If there are two things that are guaranteed to cause problems with incomers, it's the regular and liberal presence of sounds and smells that are normal, everyday occurrences in the countryside. Examples include the couple who bought a house next to the hunt kennels and then complained about the smell of cooking meat and baying hounds, or the chap who complained about the noise made by the local bikers, only to find out that the persistent roaring sounds came from the cattle in the field below his house.

You may also remember the case where an irate villager took an axe to the medieval door of the village church because she claimed she was being driven mad by the bell ringers. From the potential house buyer's point of view, if there is an old village church, then there are sure to be bells – and bell ringers. Bell ringing was a way of communicating news of a death to the community. It was generally accepted that until the 'passing bell' had been rung, the soul remained earthbound as it only 'rose to heaven on the sound of the bell.' This particular practice was stopped at the onset of WWII, when all the bells of England were silenced. For country people the sound of church bells on a summer's evening stirs pleasant memories of rural England and age-old traditions, but it might not be quite the romantic sound of bells across the meadows if you've chosen to live next door to the village church!

Animals, and livestock in particular, produce sounds and smells in large quantities. One farmer received a complaint about his sheep bleating when the lambs were sent to market. As he pointed out to the neighbour concerned, if her children were taken away she'd bleat for a while. Cows can also make the most alarming of noises. "One cow in the village was named 'the dinosaur' because it sounded like something out of Jurrasic Park when her calves were taken away," remembered one village resident. Cockerels also come pretty high on the list when it comes to neighbour disputes, simply because they don't just crow at dawn – they crow whenever they feel like it.

Good, old-fashioned, organic muck-spreading is another bone of contention between the farming community and incomers. It's the cheapest and most natural of fertilisers and has to be transported from the farmyard to the fields by wagon, which means that the road through the village can be like an oil-slick until it dries off. It makes the most appalling smell for a few days (if you live downwind) and everyone and his dog treads the slurry into the houses - but it only happens a few times during the year.

"One neighbouring farmer kept both himself and our dog amused for hours when he was muck-spreading," said one villager. "As the slurry flew out of the spreader, the dog would leap up to try and catch bits of it, which meant he was covered from head to foot in cow muck. They would keep this up for hours and if we didn't catch the dog first, he'd sneak upstairs and clean himself off on the duvet! The farmer thought all this was highly amusing and, although it was annoying, there's never been any hard feeling because he always made sure the dog was returned safely to the house when he'd finished!"

Even that most traditional of farming pursuits, hay making, has been known to elicit its own share of complaints, because people object to the wisps of hay and silage blowing off the farm wagons and into gardens as they pass through the village. And it has not been unknown for the police to be called out to 'deal with' farmers working by floodlight trying to get hay or crops in before the weather breaks.

These are all normal occurrences in village and farm life. Contrary to popular opinion the countryside is a working environment, not a theme park. This is one reason why some folk would be better off moving to a coastal or market town rather than 'a place in the country.'

First impressions.....

If you fall in love with a property at first sight, be doubly wary about the minuses. One couple were looking for a long term lease and found what they thought was the ideal spot. It was a beautiful detached house overlooking a valley, complete with fields leading down to a trout stream and miles from anywhere.

"It was perfect, an absolute dream, but there was one small snag. The landlord had retained use of a flat in a sort of annexe and, although we were assured he and his family only used it a couple of times a year, we felt there would still be a certain amount of intrusion that we didn't want. We might have coped with this except that the managing agent refused to let us have a copy of the lease for our solicitor to look at.

"From what we could gather we were having to pay double what anyone else charged for references to be taken out. The deposit, or bond, increased every year, and there was a non-negotiable year's notice should we want to leave. If for any reason we had to leave before the lease expired, we would have to pay the rent until the property was re-let. All the managing agent wanted was for us to give him a cheque so that he could take up the references 'and then we can sort it out from there.' This was non-refundable, even though he persistently ignored all our requests for information. In the finish we had to let it go and we've not found anything we've liked as much."

A family moving into a Leicestershire village couldn't see any further than their quaint cottage, only to discover that, being 'anti-hunt,' they'd moved slap-bang into the middle of an enthusiastic hunting community. The village pub, The Fox & Hounds, was the favourite haunt of hunt staff and most of the children at the village school had parents who hunted, or hunted themselves. As a result the family completely isolated themselves from their neighbours, and both sides of the divide eagerly awaited their impending move.

Problems waiting to happen.....

Wherever we move to there are always unforeseen problems waiting to happen, but we can pinpoint a few of those that are more likely to affect those new to country living. Remember that the owner of a property is under no obligation to declare any faults; the onus is on the surveyor to discover them and this depends on how thorough the surveyor is going to be, whether acting on behalf of the buyer, the seller, or the mortgage company.

When Roger and Maeve ripped up the ancient carpets and linoleum in their cottage, they discovered that all the floorboards and floor joists were rotten from the front door right through to the back and for eighteen inches up the staircase. This was because the cottage was situated near a stream and, although the property itself didn't flood, the floorboards were only inches above the damp soil. It was necessary to strip out all the floors and replace them with cement flooring which cost them a fortune.

Another family had their mother-in-law disappear through the floorboards and into a cellar the surveyor didn't even know was there. Fortunately there was no injury and the family dined out for months on the story, but problems to do with damp are not a rarity in rural properties. Older properties often have floorboards only inches above the soil where flagstones have been taken up and replaced with timber.

Bulges and cracks appearing in main walls may be caused by settlement in the foundations, or by encroaching tree roots. If there are any really large trees close to the house (in your garden, or the neighbour's), make sure that the surveyor pays particular attention to this area. By rule of thumb, tree roots spread underground, growing outwards in proportion to the overhead canopy of leaves and can have dramatic repercussions on the foundations of any nearby buildings. Thirsty trees such as poplars and especially willows will dig down into the drains, or their presence may even indicate an underground stream.

Bear in mind too that even trees in private gardens may have preservation orders placed on them, prohibiting any lopping or removal without permission from the local authority. All trees in conservation areas are automatically subject to preservation orders even though they may be causing damage to adjacent houses.

Author David Anne and his wife were forced out of the thatched cottage that had been their home for 38 years after failing to get High Court permission to fell a 120-year old lime tree. Despite the fact that a sticky, corrosive sap dripping onto the thatch of the listed cottage may have contributed to the couple's health problems, the preservation order stayed in place. Heather McCartney too caused uproar when she wanted to cut down an ancient yew which was believed to be damaging the foundations of her home.

Problems can also be caused by domestic animals and even the most conscientious of owners will find that, for a variety of reasons, livestock escapes. It may be that gates have been left open or boundaries vandalised so that sheep, cattle or horses are suddenly encountered strolling along the High Street. It's no joke to discover a flock of sheep grazing peacefully in your vegetable patch, but it can be a fact of life in the country, and it happens.

What if .....

What if the family doesn't settle? In answer to that, let's go for a worst case, but far from uncommon, scenario. Most people are usually happy enough in the beginning when everything is a novelty, but then something happens to sour the idyll and isolation and/or resentment sets in. Human nature being what it is, it is often difficult to shoulder responsibility for things going wrong and so we become angry and look for other people to blame. This is, more often than not, directed at the local folks who are accused of being stand-offish, dirty, difficult, interfering, stupid, etc.

Eventually, anger turns to bitterness because of the financial commitment made in selling up and moving to the sticks, and there is nowhere else to go. The next stage usually comes after months of trying to reverse the process by selling the property for sufficient money to be able to buy a comparable town house. The whole family is by now miserable and so desperate to get away that desperation makes them mean and spiteful as they are eventually forced to take less than what they consider a fair price. Finally, they leave it all behind with never a good word for the countryside, or the people in it. Except for the dog, who was the only one to have settled in and who decides to remain behind with the nice couple next door!

Country life doesn't suit everyone and this is why it is so important for decisions to be made for the right reasons. Thousands of people move out of the towns and cities every year looking for a more leisurely way of life – and most of them do find what they're looking for. This is where we need to refer back to the points raised in Chapter One about how and where you see the family fitting into the scheme of things. If it does make you reconsider whether you could cope in a remote farming community, or whether you'd be better off in a small market or coastal town, then we're well on the way to preventing your rural nightmare!

CHANGE OF ADDRESS

Whatever our reasons for moving to the country, it will also provide the opportunity to make other changes to our lifestyle. Allow plenty of time to sort out private possessions (ie. souvenirs, photographs, memorabilia, old sports equipment etc.), especially when leaving a family home. How much time it will take will depend on how long we've lived there, the size of the family and how much junk has been accumulated in the loft, garden shed and garage. Set a time limit for each member of the family to sort, throw out and pack their own personal belongings in boxes, which should then be clearly labelled.

If elder siblings have flown the nest but not yet settled in a permanent home (ie. at university, or gap year) make sure they are included in the sifting process so that their rubbish doesn't move with you. Otherwise, once stored in the loft at the new house, it will probably moulder there for a few more years! No doubt there will be items such as pieces of furniture that we know we will regret parting with; ask friends or relatives if they would like them on 'permanent loan,' making it clear that we may ask for them back.

The advantage of packing well in advance is that items not in daily use can be boxed and clearly labelled for unpacking at our leisure once the move is complete. Sue gave us one very sound piece of advice: "Invest in boxes of coloured labels, either for different rooms or individual owners, and put one on each side of every box because, when stacked, labels stuck on the top will not be visible. Colour co-ordination will make unpacking much simpler."

Countdown to completion.....

Once you have been given a completion date, make a provisional booking with the removal firm, but do not sign any legal agreement until the contracts on your house have actually been exchanged. While the solicitors are taking care of legal matters there are still other practical things to be taken care of. For example:

• *Finances:* even if you do not intend to move your account, you will need to notify your bank of your new address. This also applies to all savings accounts, Building Societies, Premium Bonds and National Savings.

- **Pensions/Benefits:** notify your local benefits office and give the address of your new Post Office/bank account. If your pension is paid quarterly, notify the DSS Central Pensions Branch.

- **National Insurance:** notify the appropriate department of both the old and new address, giving your National Insurance number.

- **Inland Revenue:** inform your Inspector of Taxes of the change of address.

- **Stocks & Shares:** write to the registrar and inform your financial advisor.

- **Credit Cards:** all accounts which are paid monthly by post will need to be notified, and any local charge accounts closed if you are moving out of the area.

- **Television:** check with the hire firm to see whether you can transfer the existing agreement to your new address, or whether you will be required to surrender any equipment. Notify Television Licensing and request a refund for any balance outstanding on the old property.

- **Mail Order:** selected mail order catalogues can be redirected by sending details of your change of address and quoting your personal reference number.

- **Car:** you will need to amend the address of your vehicle registration, driving licence, car insurance and any relevant motoring organisations.

- **Insurance:** personal insurers will need to be notified, together with any amendments to your contents/house insurance. Notify the insurers of your present home that the 'contents' cover should be transferred to the new address from the day you move in. Do not cancel your 'out-going' insurance cover until completion has taken place. Make sure your new house insurance cover begins on the day of completion.

- **Pets:** inform the insurance and micro-chip companies of the change of address.

- **Health Cover:** inform doctors, dentists, hospitals, clinics or day centres, the National Blood Transfusion Service and any private health care organisations.

• **Societies & Professional Organisations:** will need to be informed of new address details to update their records.

• **Memberships & Clubs:** including book, wine and sports clubs with the request to either amend or cancel membership.

• **Library:** cancel your ticket and return all books, records, etc.

• **Theatre, Concert or other Mailings:** Amend their records or cancel as appropriate.

Despite advising everyone about your change of address, there are always a few that slip through the net. The Post Office will re-direct your mail for a period of one month, three months, six months or a year on receipt of an official form and the appropriate fee. This form also has a section for notifying the National TV Licence Records Office of your change of address.

Channels of communication

Personal change of address cards can be designed on the computer, so if there is any delay in completion you will not be paying unnecessary print bills. When notifying friends and relatives it pays to make it quite clear right from the start that you will need some time to get the house straight before inviting anyone to stay.

Lewis has this warning. "Every time someone phoned to see how we were getting on, there was always a fairly unsubtle hint about them coming to stay for a weekend break. Despite the fact you've 'retired' to live in the country, there's still plenty of work to be done to make the place feel like home. People seem to be under the impression that we're on one long holiday and that we have nothing else to do other than spend hours on the telephone. They think the sheep look after themselves."

As Alexandra commented earlier, "We have to make a conscious effort not to talk 'shop' when we do have friends to visit. Additional problems stem from friends expecting to be entertained and taken out and about. Sometimes it's not possible to take a day away from the farm, especially during the lambing season or bad weather. We've known this to cause a lot of resentment. It's almost as though they think we're deliberately going out of our way to spoil their holiday, even if they've been warned beforehand that things are a bit hectic."

Jonie and Michael forestalled this problem by utilising their desktop publishing package to create their own monthly newsletter about how their settling-in programme was progressing. "Lurid details surrounding the installation of the new septic tank, complete with photographs, kept friends and family at bay for months. There's something about dodgy drains that will dissuade even the most persistent freeloader."

Bear in mind that family and friends left behind in the town are going to want to make contact more frequently, and you won't have time for letter writing. Investigate the various British Telecom packages that offer free long-distance calls after 6.oopm and during weekends as this could avoid some nasty surprises when the bill comes in. If you utilise this service, don't forget to disconnect before the hour is up and re-dial, otherwise you will be charged.

Removal firm or DIY?

"Unless you intend having a complete nervous breakdown within the first 24-hours of moving, get the professionals in," was Sue's advice. And there's a very good reason for this.....

DIY means that we have to co-ordinate everything at both ends, and if this includes kids and pets we are probably on a 'hiding to nothing' before we start. Admittedly the advantage of a DIY move is that it can save plenty on the financial front, but the cost in terms of stress may not be compensated for. The disadvantages are that it is virtually impossible to calculate van capacity to house content and the number of trips it may take. If the distance is more than 50 miles this can be uneconomical, especially if we have to make more than two trips, hire 'muscle' to help with the heavy items and return the van to its depot when we've finished.

Sue said, "A very insistent friend did our last move and at the end of the packing a very heavy slate table was left in the garden because he'd ignored the plea for this to go on first (last off). He had the nerve to suggest that we leave it behind despite the fact that it was worth well over £1000! The result was that we had to hire another van to fetch it, plus three chaps to lift it, and the resulting bill plus the original moving costs came to the same as it would have taken for a professional removal company to take the lot."

A professional removal company will pack, load and ship everything, while you and the family go on ahead, although it is a good idea for one member of the family or a friend to check that nothing is left behind in the house, garden or shed. Remember that removal companies do not generally accept responsibility for any damage to items not packed by themselves. When the estimator calls, point out any delicate, expensive or special items that may need extra attention.

If you arrange the removal for a weekend rather than a weekday, and you are moving some distance away, take into account that the main services (gas, water and electricity) will probably be closed by the time you arrive. Also, if the trip is a long one it may have to be split across two days because of the restrictions imposed on the drivers of heavy goods vehicles and the bill could also include overnight accommodation, etc. Removal firms tend to be fully booked well in advance, so you may find it easier to choose a day during the working week, in the middle of the month rather than the last weekend of the month.

Sue added, "It's no contest as far as I am concerned. Get the professionals in and drive on ahead. Book into a local B&B for a night (or even two) and at least you can have a bath without worrying about whether the hot water system or the lights are working. Moving into a strange environment is nerve racking enough without finding yourself in the arse-end of nowhere with no heating or light."

The emergency box

While all the packing and sorting is going on, take the trouble to pack an emergency box which will prevent you from tearing out your hair should you find your new destination miles away from a shop out of opening hours. This should contain a kettle and its flex; coffee, tea, sugar and longlife milk; packets of cup-a-soup; mugs, picnic plates and cutlery; a corkscrew; kitchen scissors and a tin opener; a tin of assorted biscuits; washing up liquid, cleaners and cloths; towels and soap; toilet paper; a first aid kit – especially plasters and headache tablets; candles and matches; plugs, adaptors and electrical extension leads; a torch and finally a radio.

Try to ensure that only the real essentials go in the car, especially if you are travelling with small children and pets. A long journey will be frustrating enough without members of the family having to complete the trip in cramped conditions or with their belongings on their lap. Include blankets for those who might need to sleep during the journey.

Also in the car should be a briefcase or handbag with all the family 'paperwork,' including cheque book, credit cards and a fully charged mobile phone (ideally with car charger) in case of emergency. Make sure you have a note of the telephone numbers of the solicitor, estate agent, services and the removal company's office. If the removal men have a mobile phone, take a note of the number in case either of you get separated or lost.

Moving in

Should you intend spending the first night in your new home, provision will have to be made for the bedding to be off-loaded first with the boxes clearly labelled, otherwise half the night will have gone before you locate the duvet. Requirements will, of course, depend on the size of the family, but the children will probably enjoy a night of 'camping out' on the floor. Just make sure there are plenty of blankets and sleeping bags to cushion the bare boards, as these can become extremely hard after a few hours.

Similarly, food needs to be taken into account. Adults can often cope with a sandwich on the move, but with a family it may be a good idea to picnic, unless a cooker (camping or otherwise) is fully functioning on your arrival. In fact, a portable gas camping stove should be considered an essential for country living as, in some remote parts, the electricity goes off with depressing regularity – and don't forget a supply of gas canisters.

Unless we have already decided where our belongings are going and everything is clearly marked on the boxes, it's a good idea to get the removal company to pile all the boxes into one room. Better still, if your new country home has a dry, secure barn, have everything dumped out there and sort through it at your leisure after everywhere has had a thoroughly good clean. Large kitchen appliances and heavy pieces of furniture, however, should be moved by people who know how to move them, and left in situ.

Covering all eventualities

One of the most important things to remember when moving into the depths of the country is that the nearest DIY store could be twenty miles or more away, and the local hardware store will close promptly at 5.30pm for the entire weekend. If you arrive late on Saturday or any time on Sunday, there probably won't be anywhere open for screws, light bulbs, nails, rawlplugs etc., so an assortment of all of these should be located next to the tool kit which in turn should go in the car so that the electric drill, screwdrivers, fuse wire, hammers etc. are immediately to hand upon arrival. Work on the principle of Murphy's Law that anything that can go wrong will go wrong and include repair kits for everything.

The parsimony of people leaving a house usually includes the removal of every single light bulb in the place, especially the energy-saving long-life variety, although the exception will be some dim, dusty 40 watt orb in the downstairs lavatory. Take a selection of functioning light bulbs rather than fancy ones.

Bring extension leads too, because no socket will be convenient for the electric drill or be located where you want them, and a small set of steps, otherwise you could be heading for a fall if you rely on some wobbly chair the previous owners have left behind.

Stress management

We all have our own methods for dealing with stress, and moving house is supposed to be one of the most stressful events in a person's life. With the best will in the world, tempers will flare, tantrums will manifest themselves, and by the time the first 24 hours have passed most of the family will have expressed the sentiment that they wished they'd never left the old house.

Martin and Chris have moved several times and have the following suggestion. "Make sure your survival kit has a bottle of Bach's Rescue Remedy for dogs and children, and a chill box with several half bottles of champagne and a couple of glasses for yourself!"

This is often why it is a good idea to stop at a local B&B or hotel for a couple of nights. At least everyone can get away from the chaos and have a bath and a hot meal before settling down for a good night's sleep. If it's a family business and arrangements have been made well in advance, the welcoming warmth may even be extended to the family dog, who will also be suffering from stress and over-excitement.

Coping with children

With children of any age the sense of novelty and adventure will quickly wear off. Actively encourage older children to involve themselves in the planning and decoration of their new rooms and try not to criticise the proposed décor, even if the visualisation of the finished room makes your eyes water. This is another reason why coloured stickers for each member of the family are just as important as different colours for each room. Children can then be given the task of carting their own boxes up to their rooms.

Needless to say, young children will become tired and fractious, not to mention hungry, long before their parents are ready to pack it in for the day. Do make sure that none of the children wander off alone because the countryside does have its dangerous elements: a stream swollen by recent rain, reversing farm traffic and unfamiliar animals can present a risk for any unaccompanied toddlers. Keep the family together at all times (including the dog) until you have all had the opportunity to explore and become familiar with your new surroundings.

Coping with pets

We have to realise that moving home can be just as stressful for pets, especially as people often give a tremendous amount of thought to the family dog when actually choosing a new house. And there are, of course, all sorts of problems to face when moving pets to a new home. Sometimes it might be better to kennel while the move is in progress, but this will depend on the distance between the old home and the new and may not be practical. Dogs enjoy the thrill of new places, although they are equally prone to upset during the packing period. Make sure he doesn't get caught up with the excitement of all the activity and then runs off while the removal men are constantly in and out of the house – this applies both at the old address and the new one.

Cats present far more of a problem since it will be necessary to keep them shut in the house for several days before moving and for at least 48 hours after the move. Select one room at the new house that can be shut off from all the activity and put the cat in there with food, water, a litter tray and a cushion or coat with a familiar smell on it. At the end of the day when everyone is in for the night, let the cat out of the room, making sure all the doors and windows are closed. Try to keep the cat in for at least two days before letting it outside, and then only do this just before feeding time. Cats are sensitive creatures and may need a medicinal tin of pilchards or tuna to convince them that life is still worth living.

Jayne remembers: "Poor old Cass got the squitters with all the upheaval and twenty minutes after the cat basket had been put in the car, he erupted. The stench was appalling but we couldn't risk getting him out in case he ran off. It was a very depressed looking moggy who came out at the other end some four hours later. It took days to clean him up because he was so deeply offended by it all."

Small caged birds and other small pets such as mice, guinea pigs, rabbits and hamsters should be transported in secure, draught-proof containers. Remove all toys but make sure that they have access to both food and water in non-spill containers because it's quite easy to overlook their needs during the chaos of moving. One cage wasn't secure enough as Rob discovered. He recalled, "When we got to the other end there was a cage but no ferrets. We eventually found them curled up at the back of the furniture lorry, inside one of the boxes of cushions. They obviously felt it was a better way to travel."

Your new life

Well, you're here now and the removal lorry has disappeared round the bend. There are crates and boxes all over the place, noone can find the kettle flex and the dog is now lying down in a darkened room with a damp flannel on his forehead. This is, as they say, the first day of the rest of your life, so pull on your wellies and go outside to greet the world – even if it is pouring with rain and the smell of silage is over-powering.

INTEGRATION OR ALIENATION?

When the town moves to the country it can find rural etiquette confusing, if not a veritable minefield. Two books spring to mind which might lessen the chance of making social gaffe after social gaffe. These are *The Farmer Wants A Wife* by Maeve Haran and *Any Fool's Country Life* by James Robertson (originally published separately as *Any Fool Can Be A Countryman* and *Any Fool Can Be A Villager*).

Author Maeve Haran recalls being invited to a supper party after moving to her weekend cottage. Decking herself out in her usual finery, she arrived to find that the host opened the door in jeans and socks. "The other guests were similarly dressed. Even though everyone was wonderfully welcoming, I spent the rest of the evening cringing because I looked so over the top." After that she witnessed and committed enough gaffes to write a book about them.

Let's make no bones about it: some country folk can be almost as hostile as the hillbillies confronted by Burt Reynolds in *Deliverance* - and just as good an aim with a rifle! "I was horrified by what almost amounted to blatant racism when we moved into the village," said one newcomer. "You half expect that sort of reaction in the inner cities, but noone warned us that country people could be so prejudiced against townies. Our neighbouring farmer would pass me in the lane with a curt nod, making it quite plain that he didn't invite further communication."

So how do we get it right?

Re-inventing yourself

Okay, agreed there are some ridiculous people who pretend to a much deeper affinity with country life than they have any right to. And there are those who parade around in pristine 4x4 vehicles and brand new Barbours on their way to the weekend cottage. But there are others who live in the major towns and cities whose attachment to rural life is totally sincere. Many were born and bred in the country and moved to the town in pursuit of a career; they describe themselves in a low key manner as "someone who knows how to behave in the country."

An acquaintance with genuine rural origins wistfully observed that as a weekender you do miss out on a lot of the 'hunting and farming gossip,' but he still makes no pretence at being a full time countryman. Julian Seaman, who lectured on fashion design at St. Martin's School for Art in London, and also rode in the British three-day event team, would always go to the country to ride. "All my riding career I commuted to my horses out of London, which was rather nice. I kind of had the best of both worlds."

Having moved into her country cottage, Rosemary resisted the urge to erect high fences between her and her neighbour's garden. As a result they eventually chatted over the garden fence and when she goes away on business, her neighbour has offered to feed the cat and water the plants.

Friction between incomers, particularly the 'weekenders,' and locals is nothing new, but due to the previous decade's property boom, it has become more widespread and, according to a Daily Telegraph report, increasingly divisive. As journalist Tessa Boase wrote: "It's not so much the rocketing prices and empty villages that make the locals despise you. What really winds them up is your behaviour when visiting. Because no matter how much you like to think of that Norfolk farmhouse as 'home' and the Islington pad as a pied-à-terre, the reality is that weekenders remain visitors." Integration is the key - right from the start.

Fools rush in

Country people cope quite happily with eccentricity, but they are not so tolerant of affectation, or indeed being patronised. Neither do they take kindly to complaints about activities that have been going on for centuries. Jennifer recalls a supper party during a visit to some old friends who'd just moved to the country. Her husband began by airing his views on blood sports and the whole table went quiet. Jennifer aimed a kick at him under the table so he headed off down the equally tricky avenue of farming subsidies and it went even quieter. There was an arctic wind blowing by the time he enthused over how cheap the house prices were in the area. Jennifer was so mortified by this demonstration of social suicide that she knocked a glass of red wine straight down the front of the hostess's white cashmere sweater. "Needless to say, we haven't been invited back....or anywhere else for that matter. Whenever we go down for a visit, we're kept well away from their new chums."

Visitors to the country often echo 'green' sentiments that British farmers should not be looking to make a profit from farming. They should, it appears, be focussing on the one thing that now matters in the countryside - the environment. As James Douglas remarked acidly in Country Illustrated: "This writer has obviously been under the naïve and ignorant misapprehension that, in the course of doing their work and running their businesses, farmers did not make a bad job of looking after the environment." He went on to reflect that generations of farming families had obviously laboured under the misguided belief that when it came to providing the nation with a rural landscape, they hadn't done too bad a job.

Unfortunately, all too often the urban reader is misinformed by publications that offer seductive solutions to complex issues and rely on a carefully cultivated imagery to avert any awkward questions. There appears to be little thought given to the men who put their money into the land and, hopefully, make a profit from their labours and pass it on so that their succeeding sons and daughters can do the same, always with the hope of making enough money to support future generations. "For a storekeeper to open a shop with the avowed intention of doing anything other than making a profit would seem absurd. Why should farmers be any different?" asks Douglas.

One incomer pushed invitations through the doors of all the neighbours in the village, summoning them all for drinks on the following Saturday evening. "Our village is made up completely of farming or local people, except for a couple of weekend cottages, and we all decided we'd go along, more out of curiosity than good manners," confessed a guest. "A group of us arrived at 7.30 sharp and were greeted at the door by a chap wearing a dress.....it was later explained that this was a sarong like David Beckham wore, but it was a bit disconcerting for a group of middle-aged, dyed-in-the-wool Welsh farmers to be welcomed by a grizzled, six-foot string bean with a beard and wearing a frock!"

Another countryman objects to regular tours offered by incomers when entertaining visiting friends. Sitting outside a local pub with some friends after watching an afternoon of village cricket, they were treated to a loud voice braying, "What on earth have they done to your village, Brigit? There are cars everywhere. You really must complain to the council."

It's where you do your shopping that counts

In any country village the closure of the shop and Post Office can be disastrous, especially for the elderly and those without transport. Like the church, the pub or the parish magazine, it is a focal point of village life and the place where we make first contact with the locals.

Unfortunately, for those used to urban megastores, many village shops are considered to be behind the times; they don't stock goods or brands that incomers want and can be drastically over-priced. More and more, these small family concerns are being forced out of business simply because the turnover no longer covers the running costs. The shop and Post Office in a Wiltshire village found itself in such a position when the proprietor announced her retirement, but the villagers rallied round and formed a 'village shop association.' The shop's landlord made the magnanimous gesture of offering a five-year lease when he could possibly have sold the site for development.

Out of 300 people on the parish's electoral roll 170 brought shares, while others pledged loans from £5 to £500, and within five weeks they had raised enough money to re-stock and re-decorate. A handful of volunteers now man the counters on a regular basis and there is a steady stream of customers going in and out. On top of the face-lift, the chairman of the parish council applied to the Countryside Agency for funds from the Vital Villages scheme and received a grant of £21,500 towards the venture.

Country weekender and food writer Rose Prince commented: "I hate going to supermarkets because, if you know farmers and people who make food not just through work but socially, you know how badly they are ripped off by supermarkets. Farmers near us have been ruined by supermarkets.....they get a pittance for a litre of milk which sells for a high profit in the supermarket."

Agreed, the village shop may be more expensive and carry a smaller range of goods, but it pays in the long run to do at least part of our weekly shopping locally, even if it's only vegetables and meat from the farm shop and eggs from a neighbouring farmer. And if we live in a rural area without a shop or Post Office, or if they are being threatened with closure, it might be worth contacting Rural Community Shops (formerly Virsa), a Dorset-based charity supported by the Plunkett Foundation which helps to 're-energising rural retail services.' This organisation has helped more than 800 villages and has established about 40 community shops and Post Offices in England and Wales. They encourage local people to form village associations in order to buy or rent a property, and to run the shop and Post Offices themselves. They are now helping to support the survival of many threatened rural pubs too.

"My first port of call was the local shop," remembers Barbara, "and the reason for this was two-fold. Firstly, working from home and living alone, I wanted to work out how much travelling I needed to do to shop for myself each week, and secondly, I wanted to be seen to be supporting the village if I was going to settle there. As it happens, I can get most of what I want from the shop and do a major Tesco trip once a month. Milk, meat, eggs, papers, vegetables and bread are all now delivered to the door."

Fund raising

A lot of fund raising goes on in villages and many of the local ladies have raised 'tin-rattling' to an art form. In fact, there's not a lot that goes on locally that hasn't been supported by the villagers who dig deep into their pockets to pledge whatever support they can afford.

Alli explained, "We support just about everything and even if we can't afford a donation, items for raffle prizes are just as well received. We don't go to church, but the vicar knows he can count on us to give something to help his fund raising. It's all about community and the children are included in anything that goes on in the village."

Lloyd, however, is not always supportive of Lucy's fund raising efforts. "We always seem to be cluttered up with people I wouldn't normally want as dinner guests, and so I tend to remain in London until the latest fund raising project is out of the way. Lucy's friends are mainly the horsey crowd and she's grown up with most of them, so I'm really superfluous to requirements in that department."

Unlike urban fund raising, village collections are usually to support many grass roots activities that are not always publicised, but which are very close to home. Roger and Maeve had been in the village for less than a year when a bag containing some groceries and a £5 note in an envelope was left on their doorstep during Christmas week. Fearing that the bag had been left at the wrong address they took it to the local postmistress who explained that as they were pensioners within the parish, it was a gift from the village pensioners' fund. "This automatic inclusion was a bit of a surprise," said Roger, "but this and other discreet gestures made us realise how important it was for us to support other fund raising efforts."

Footpaths and bridle ways

When buying a property it is advisable to look closely at the footpaths and bridle ways that cross either your land or any adjoining farmland because this means that people have the legal entitlement to walk or ride past your home.

"We've completely changed our attitudes to the 'right to roam' policy," explained Stephen, who moved to a local firm of solicitors from a large town. "When disputes appeared in the news, we'd always thought 'For goodness sake, what harm does it do?' but having a footpath about 100 yards from our house has put a different slant on the subject. At weekends, from April to September, we are regularly confronted by a posse of orange and blue anoraks who have got lost and have decided to use our garden and drive as a short cut back to the main road, even though there is no right of way."

"Sometimes it can be very creepy to have complete strangers lurking about when I'm at home on my own," added Chris. "It wouldn't be so bad if there was an apology but they seem to think it's their god-given right to trample over someone else's property without a 'by your leave,' when they've no right to be there. I don't want strangers around when the children are outside playing, it makes me nervous."

Jayne and Tony lived in a secluded bungalow at the end of a lane which led to a public footpath across the fields opposite their home. "A local 'treasure hunt' would frequently use this route, which was fine, except that they would bang on the door at any time during a weekend or summer evening to ask for directions. The fact that there was a 'Keep Out' notice on the front gate did not deter them in the slightest, but when we acquired a rather volatile and unpredictable corgi from the rescue centre, he did!"

Footpaths originate from tracks used by local people to take short cuts to neighbouring farms, villages, churches or places of work, but constant use over generations now makes them a public right of way.

This means that the public has the right of access to use the footpath: it does not mean free-ranging over the field, or allowing dogs to run about off the lead. Bridle paths have a similar origin but are designated for the use of riders – and in the country referring to 'riding' means horses, not mountain bikes or any other form of mechanised transport!

Note: never refer to 'horseback riding' or you'll get a blank stare that asks, "What else would you ride?"

Modernised or brutalised?

Local people are extremely protective of what they see as their heritage. For over 200 years the unspoilt village of Selborne in Hampshire had been regarded as one of the most beautiful in the country. That was until a local landowner, with a grant from DEFRA (often referred to locally as the Department for the Eradication of Farming & Rural Affairs), began digging up parts of the village in order to 'improve' the landscape. This environmental improvement involved mechanical diggers ripping chunks out of the water meadows to create three man-made ponds in the name of 'bio-diversity.'

Neither will there be much local support for the concept of the '21st century village' like the one built in Cambridgeshire, which caters for those who want the 'villagey feel' without having to run the gauntlet of getting on with the locals. In this instance the locals objected to having an 'instant settlement' of 10,000 people plus a business park being built on a greenfield site. They managed to delay planning permission for twelve years before the first bulldozers went in, but 'progress' had its way in the end. As a result it is the residents of genuine Domesday villages and whose cottages jut out into country lanes who have to suffer the commuter rat-runs.

For most country people one of the most horrific sights in the landscape is that architectural monstrosity, the barn conversion. After decades of transforming every type of agricultural building into a dwelling, the powers-that-be finally decided that barns should remain barns, and have finally pulled the plug on planning permission for any further developments. Unfortunately architects are never forced to live in the houses they create, and few appear to appreciate the difference between modernising and brutalising.

Up until a few years ago there were still plenty of derelict rural properties that were desperately in need of renovation, but these are now few and far between. When Stewart found his ideal home he was appalled at the architect's plans for the rebuilding of the cottage. "The end product would have finished up looking more like a pub than a home. There wasn't a lot of room, even though it was just for me and Jake [his dog], but the open plan bar-room style wasn't me. Perhaps the architect thought a recently divorced, single chap – think 'blokey' – when all I wanted was to keep things as traditional as possible."

Often it's the newcomers themselves who create 'exclusion zones' around their homes. There are frequent reports in the newspapers about wealthy celebrity owners complaining about there being no contact with their neighbours after having erected a seven-foot high wall with electric security gates on a property to which most local people were probably used to having access. To be included in village activities the organisers like to know that their invitations will not be ignored or dismissed out of hand. Ignore them at your peril, or you may just find that the village's own exclusion measures are even more effective than high walls and security gates!

The grapevine

The grapevine, Chinese whispers or the bush telegraph: call it what you will, there is nothing like it anywhere else for spreading gossip

– even if it's total fabrication. Anyone who has sat and watched just a few episodes of Emmerdale will see how gossip and rumour thrives in a small rural community. Every village has its Edna or Betty, malicious matriarchs who will invent or embellish a story to maintain their reputations as the local oracle.

"Some of these women are downright evil," said Margaret. "Let the shopkeeper deliver the box of Oxo cubes that you left on the counter by mistake at nine, and you'll both be embroiled in a passionate affair by noon."

The irony is that although everyone knows these are notorious gossips, it doesn't prevent the rumours from spreading. Martin and Chris are a gay couple who have experienced all manner of difficulties when it comes to integrating into village life. Although they run an extremely popular country restaurant, they don't find their neighbours very welcoming. "The wives are okay, but the husbands are nervous," said Chris. "In the country it's all action man stuff, and almost as if they feel their chums might think it highly suspect if they were too friendly with us. Having said that, they've just discovered that Martin can shoot the eye out of a clay pigeon at any distance, and the thaw seems to be setting in."

"As far as the gossips are concerned, I think homosexuality is outside the sphere of reference for elderly ladies," added Martin. "The best they have been able to come up with are vague references to drugs and Nöel Coward, but we await further developments with interest."

Be warned that in a village, gossip never completely goes away. "I can remember my grandmother regularly making a comment about an elderly widow, 'She had to get married, you know'," said Sue. "My grandmother was in her late nineties and the neighbour only fractionally younger, but this little bit of gossip would be wheeled out whenever the poor woman's name was mentioned. This misdemeanour must have happened nearly seventy years earlier and probably hadn't a grain of truth in it, but it was always accompanied by pursed lips and a knowing look."

Don't call us.....

Very often neighbours won't bother to get involved with new people because they know they're going to leave eventually, especially when it comes to tenanted property. Carol's stand-offish neighbour isn't an isolated instance. Villagers have discovered that newcomers are a transient bunch and that few are willing to put down tap roots in the community; one Welsh village reckoned on a five year turn-around and they weren't far wrong in their calculations.

When villagers' families have lived there for generations, they have a completely different perspective from the Chelsea tractor brigade, who look upon property as a financial investment rather than a life-long commitment. Added to this, newcomers are often seen as 'pushy' and interfering when it comes to village business, even if that's not the intention – what a newcomer may see as an offer to help may, more often that not, be seen by the locals as a take-over bid!

Many people retiring to the country still keep themselves to themselves. As a result in many of the out-lying villages there are rows of bungalows full of widows who don't even know their neighbours. "They started off coming as second home owners and didn't bother to make friends because they had their husbands. Now they don't know anyone," explained one villager. "It wasn't us that kept them out."

A little bit of mystery does no harm.....and the latest family moving into a village provides enough speculation to keep everyone going for a month, but it does pay to keep our distance and not rush in to any confessions or revelations. Village folk are wary and easily spooked, so keep things on a purely civil footing for the first few weeks, or even months. Plenty of exchanges of normal civilities will thaw the ice quicker than rushing about trying to be too friendly – it doesn't work that way.

Like the Palace, the village likes to make the first move, as Jim and Trish found. "We were too busy to talk to people when we moved in, but we made a point of acknowledging all the neighbours whenever we met. One day we'd asked about the nearest hire place for equipment because we needed a rotavator for the garden. The next thing we knew, a chap had turned up with one on the back of his tractor saying we could borrow it for as long as we liked. I think the secret is that perhaps people like to see you doing things yourself, rather than just spending a lot of money on renovations."

Although John was a local farmer, his new wife Jackie was in publishing and worked in London, the couple having met in a classic *Four Weddings and a Funeral* scenario. "Farmers don't have time for much of a social life, and what with commuting and everything, I'd rarely spoken to half a dozen people in six months," she recalls. "It wasn't until the WI wanted to produce a local history that my sister-in-law informed them of my publishing connections. The book gave us a common interest and I've begun to be included in village activities whenever I'm at home."

John, however, believes his wife's rather glamorous image put neighbours off. "Jackie is a striking looking girl but all they saw was her driving through the village in a natty little sports car. I think she was a bit of a mystery.....and still is, I must say. Having said that, I'm glad my sister made the effort, because I was worried Jackie might never settle in, and would want to go back to London."

Stewart experienced quite the opposite. "As soon as it was known that there was a single, half presentable chap in the village, I was snowed under with invitations. I'd had a messy divorce and the last thing I wanted was to be the 'spare man' at every social gathering, so I developed the tragic mask and very gently, but politely, declined. Keeping yourself to yourself doesn't mean being stand-offish, although it does create an element of mystery, which they'd all like to solve. I'd never had so many offers from neighbours to walk the dog while I was at work!"

.....but having a sense of humour helps

Humour can get people out of the trickiest of situations and it does pay to have a sense of humour when wires get crossed. Rather than seeing villagers as a bunch of swede-bashing yokels when misunderstandings arise, try to view things with a far less jaundiced eye. When town meets country there are bound to be teething problems, but one solution is learning to laugh and not take life too seriously.

LIVESTOCK AND LOCALS

It is also a good time to reflect on what we mean by the countryside. For a healthy natural balance it is necessary for British farming to be more than just the maintenance of a landscape that people like to look at and walk in. It is an accepted fact that two thirds of agricultural land is pasture – ie. grassland. Left to its own devices, land will quickly regress to scrub and, ultimately, reforestation. If grass is not maintained on a large scale by the grazing of animals, it will not remain grass for very long.

If a house stands empty for a period of time, the lawn will quickly degenerate into anthills, twitch grass and tree seedlings, often within the space of a year. Once farmland ceases to be farmed, it will soon become a tangle of brambles and other intrusive cover. The only way in which the necessary grazing can be provided is by livestock farming and only large grazing animals can fulfill this need. Many would like to see livestock farming disappear from the landscape – which is rather an insult to our ancestors, both two and four legged, who struggled to drag civilisation out of the forest.

"We had a group of pagan folk move into one of the houses, and it wasn't long before they started telling us how wrong livestock farming was," said one farmer. "According to them, all the animals should be allowed to roam free, since there was no need to kill them for food. They couldn't grasp that if cattle weren't in the fields to be reared for meat, then there wouldn't be any sheep or cattle anywhere in the landscape. This sort of cloud cuckoo land philosophy is best kept in the towns where it belongs, and won't win anybody any friends round here."

The countryside is where people live and make a living, either through agriculture or livestock, and while there will always be bad farmers, they are in the minority. Those who have been farming the land for generations do not need advice on animal rights, welfare or liberation, and it only fuels ill-feeling if those expressing such opinions do so without any personal, first-hand knowledge, or experience of land management. Don't be afraid to ask questions, but keep those pre-formed opinions to yourself until you've had the opportunity to get to know more about the countryside and those who work it.

If it's got fur or feathers—it bites

It's also a good idea to keep in mind that in the countryside, even the mildest mannered of creatures will react if it's not handled or approached correctly. In the lifestyle magazines psychologists are always explaining how to read the body language of our friends and colleagues – well, country people do the same with their livestock. Because they know when an animal is likely to be aggressive or a touch menopausal, they steer clear of the field or paddock until the danger is past.

It pays to remember that despite the campaign to publicise the countryside as a ramblers' paradise, domestic animals don't read the small print. If we want to walk across an open field when the bull has been turned out with the heifers, then be ready to break into a sprint should he decide to lower his head and charge. Sheep and pigs with young can also be pretty aggressive – and even a shortcut through the farmyard could offend the sensibilities of a territorial cockerel or sheepdog. If we do decide to wander off the designated footpaths and on to private land, then we must be prepared for the consequences.

Sheep: There was the well-publicised incident that caused a great deal of mirth when a contestant at the Leeds International Piano Festival was assaulted by a sheep during his relaxation period. The commentators felt it was highly hilarious and incongruous that a sheep should be the perpetrator of such an indignity, but sheep have their moments too, especially during the lambing season.

Cattle: When a farmer went to investigate why a group of his bullocks were huddled in the corner of the field, he found a middle-aged lady and her dog perched precariously on the lower branches of a tree. Cattle are inquisitive creatures and a whole herd breaking into a run can be an alarming sight. Another dog walker had to undergo four hours of surgery after being trampled by a herd of 35 cows.

Horses: As herd animals, horses will instinctively react to the rest breaking into a wild gallop across the field, especially if there is a dog loose. Most horses are good natured, but those that have the urge to bite can inflict a nasty wound given half a chance.

Pigs: An enraged sow protecting her young will attack a human and is capable of inflicting fatal injuries. Don't be fooled by the public image of the Tamworth Two!

Goats: Even those that have been de-horned can knock a fully-grown man off his feet. They are immensely strong and incredibly stubborn, which does not always bode well for the naïve would-be goat keeper.

Chickens: Cockerels can be some of the most vicious creatures encountered in the farmyard. They are possessed of innate cunning and strike fear into the hearts of service callers such as postmen and meter readers.

Another example of animals not behaving according to human expectations was recorded in The Countryman's Weekly, explaining why a docile pet ferret can turn into a wild animal once it starts working. Simply because below ground there are not only rabbits, but also rats, stoats, weasels or even foxes, instinct kicks in and immediately the animal is on the defensive. When it resurfaces it may be excited, angry or even wounded – and this is where body language comes in; you go to pick the ferret up without understanding this and it turns to bite. "Remember that the ferret has just been on another planet. It thinks it is being attacked and defends itself."

Even a pet rabbit can cut up rough and those powerful back legs with their long claws can inflict a nasty wound, as one pet owner recalls: "We bought a rabbit for the children, but he turned out to be so vicious that no-one could get near him. He took to living wild in the garden, and on several occasions I had to go and apologise to neighbours because the damn thing had savaged their cat or dog. It must have been one very lucky bunny, because he actually died of old age. I don't think there was a fox in the neighbourhood who would tackle him!"

The class(less) system

Don't think that money will impress anyone in the country: classlessness starts in primary school, as one newly arrived family found out. "There's a wider age range in each class and across wider social groups," said Laura, "and parents get to know each other very quickly. I was talking to a very pleasant woman for ages when I went to pick up the children. I didn't know until weeks later that she was married to one of the biggest landowners in the county, but you'd never have known. She treats me like.....well, like I'm just the same as herself."

Michael was waiting to be served in the local shop and was idly listening to the bitchy speculation about the ownership of a brand new Land Rover that was parked outside. "The customers were an assorted bunch, mostly us incomers after the Sunday papers," he said. "You could almost feel the mental calculations about who would be the first to court the prestigious new money that had obviously arrived in the village. There was a wonderfully embarrassing silence when the owner turned out to be a decrepit old local farmer who'd been in the queue and heard every word."

"My mother was often rebuked by the new owner of the local chemist shop where she worked, for 'encouraging' conversation with a rather smelly, tatty woman customer. Her clothes were held together with bailing twine and she kept her money in a battered tobacco tin," remembers one villager. "What he didn't know was that she was one of the wealthiest landowners in the area, and that she and my mother had gone to the same private girls' school together."

The village idiot

A good, politically incorrect topic, but every village has one, and they are not half as silly as they like to appear, like the story of the simple Welsh lad who hung around a film crew who were staying at the local pub. The director announced that he needed a dead fox for the next day's shooting and could anyone help. The lad piped up that he could provide the necessary body and the fee was agreed at £25. Next morning the dead fox was duly delivered and at the end of the day the lad was required to get rid of it.

Some hours later the director turned up on the doorstep and explained that the film needed to be shot again and that he'd need another fox. The lad scratched his head but allowed himself to be persuaded to obtain another for a further fee of £25. The fox was duly delivered and at the end the lad again disposed of it, as requested.

The director decided that he could use the fox in yet another shot, so he approached the lad again, but this time the price had gone up to £50 due to the growing shortage of foxes in the locality. What the film director didn't know was that the lad had remembered seeing a road kill which he had dumped in his mother's freezer overnight, fluffing up the fur with her hair dryer the next morning.

Later, over a pint in the pub, the film director made some comment about the lad being a bit simple. "Oh, I dunno about that," said the Welshman standing next to him. "He's made a hundred quid selling you the same dead fox three times over, so he can't be that daft, can he?"

Making the right approach is keeping your distance

One couple found themselves cold-shouldered because they had inadvertently stepped on villagers' toes by persistently volunteering their services to various local committees. Within no time at all they found themselves ignored in the local social club, treated like aliens when they attended a summer fete and were later shunned at the Christmas Village Dance! "Talking to people here is like trying to get blood out of a stone and there's no way you can make eye contact. You just can't break into conversation with anyone."

Incomers volunteering for various committees in the country are more likely to be seen as 'pushy' by the locals, so wait for the invitation. If you have specific interests or talents, drop this information in casually while chatting in the Post Office – it will filter through to the right person much more effectively than you trying to make contact directly. Local folk might not want the job themselves, but they'll soon object to new people making what they see as a take-over bid and interfering in village affairs!

Sheila is a talented flower arranger, but when she moved into the village she merely offered to supply flowers from her garden for the ladies who do the flowers in the church. Regardless of where you live, the flower ladies' province is a minefield, regardless of how hideous the arrangements might be, but Sheila knew this. Impressed by the arrangements they saw when collecting the weekly flower supply ensured that Sheila was quickly invited to join the team. It was now their idea, you see?

Free range animals and children

One thing guaranteed to cause friction between country folk and incomers is a roaming dog – and for dogs used to an urban environment, a flock of sheep can be a tempting sight. Up to a few years ago gamekeepers and farmers shot roaming dogs on sight, but such drastic action would undoubtedly result in legal repercussions today. Farmers who shoot straying dogs now have to prove damage to livestock, and that they had no alternative but to kill the marauders.

That said, a dog doesn't need to savage sheep to cause financial losses to a farmer. Sheep are hysterical animals at the best of times and a playful dog can cause ewes to abort or even die simply by chasing them. To the dog, with no malice aforethought, it may seem like a wonderful game, but it can turn out to be an extremely costly one for you.

Straying dogs don't have to worry livestock to cause a nuisance. A young sheepdog that sat beneath his window and howled visited one local resident almost nightly. The moment it heard the back door open it scarpered – until the next night. By nefarious planning worthy of the SAS, the sheepdog was eventually captured and handed over to the local dog warden. The outcome was that the dog was claimed by a farmer who lived a couple of miles away – his excuse for the dog straying was that he couldn't keep it shut in at night because all it did was howl until the next morning!

Unfortunately, there is still a firm non-neutering policy amongst farmers when it comes to dogs and cats, especially working animals. This has a serious knock-on effect with the number of unwanted (or unplanned) kittens and puppies that are produced every year; rescue sanctuaries are bulging with collie-crosses and boxes of kittens. If the family decide on adopting one of these 'orphans' there shouldn't be a problem, but adult rescue dogs can be among the most difficult animals to train if you are not an experienced 'dog person.'

"I wouldn't have anything else other than a rescue dog," said Sue, "and I'll always go for a lurcher or greyhound, which can mean double-difficulty. As it happens, I'm familiar with the breed and all its little idiosyncrasies, but they do need some keeping up with due to a basic innate cunning that is constantly trying to outwit you. And they are not known as 'dinner snatchers' for nothing, either!"

Annie and Paul took their rescued Great Dane, Gus, with them and he had no trouble in settling down, until a neighbour's terrier bitch came into season. For a week he refused to eat and lay outside in the cold underneath his lady-friend's window, the silence of the village only broken by long periodic drawn-out and mournful howls.

Scamp, on the other hand, was more resourceful: a small, nippy fox terrier, the biggest difficulty was keeping him out. That little dog would scale walls and clamber in bathroom windows if the object of his desire was on the inside. Scamp was a local character and fathered more litters of puppies than any other dog in the neighbourhood until he was hit by a passing car while his mind was probably distracted by other things.

On a more serious note, taking an urban dog to the countryside can be a recipe for disaster if we haven't made sure all our boundaries are secure. In a small community, owning a dog that isn't under proper control is not going to win any support from the neighbours – and neither are free range children. It is also very important to keep children under control. Farmland is not a theme park or adventure playground; it is a place of work and there are dangers for those unfamiliar with the environment. Providing children show respect for a farmer's property and livestock, it could only be a matter of months before they have won the neighbour over completely – but access to farmland is not ours by right.

One of the quickest ways to fall out with the local farmer is to allow both dogs and children to rampage over his land without first asking permission. Despite the accusations of groups representing the ramblers, walkers and hikers, farmers rarely object to local people walking across their land: what they do object to is the cavalier attitude of what they refer to as the 'boots and rucksack' brigade, who seem to think it is their 'right' to go where they please, irrespective of whether the land is private property or not, and to allow dogs to run loose among livestock. Make a point of asking the farmer if it's okay to walk the dog on his land.....we've never had a refusal.

Acquiring livestock

"It's the easiest thing in the world to acquire livestock, and the most difficult to get rid of," remarked one long-suffering smallholder. The countryside abounds with helpful people who all seem to know someone who can let you have all manner of livestock for a 'fiver' – which generally means that it wouldn't fetch that amount at a farmers'mart.

One couple attended a poultry sale and put in a bid for a crate of what appeared to be young point-of-lay hens. They got them home only to discover that the crate contained a selection of game cockerels, which don't always have large, distinctive combs.

For the fledgling countryman, steer well clear of the mart unless you know what you are buying or have an experienced person with you. And if you do go to the mart, leave the kids at home. Caged animals can look extremely forlorn and you'll come home with all sorts of creatures that will only cost you a lot of money to keep. No matter what you've been told, livestock doesn't live on grass alone!

When to say 'no'

Ask for advice by all means, but still don't be too eager to agree to take on any stock unseen. When Barbara announced that she wanted some laying hens one local farmer wasn't slow in coming forward. "A big box arrived and money changed hands, but when we tipped them out you'd never seen such a motley assortment of birds," she remembers. "Even to my inexperienced eye, they were long past their sell-by date. One bird was a scruffy, rangy old thing with only one eye, so God knows how old she was when I got her. As it happened, Flopsy Chicken survived the lot and I kept her for 10 years, so how old she was when she died I'd hate to think."

Annie wanted a pygmy goat as a pet and one day a neighbour turned up with a delightful little nanny. "She was such a delicate little thing," she recalls. "Tiny hooves, big curious eyes and a pair of horns that gave her a cute Walt Disney look. In no time at all this pretty little kid turned into a huge monster, and it took us all our time to handle her because those horns could dish out a painful jab if she was feeling stubborn. We loved Flossie, but oh, how we dreaded her next escapade. She cornered the vicar in the telephone box on the green and delivered an amazing coup de grace on the local Master of Foxhounds!"

The fox and the hen house

For most newcomers the first livestock they acquire usually manifests itself in the form of half a dozen hens – which quickly become family pets, all with names and identities. The family take a great deal of pleasure from the hens milling around and producing fresh eggs for breakfast. Then the unthinkable happens. Our youngest goes up to collect the eggs and discovers the mangled bodies and feathers all over the place – and not a hen in sight. Suffice to say, a fox's rampage in the hen house has altered quite a lot of perceptions about this controversial creature.

If foxes become a problem, trapping and snaring are allowed, but far more landowners these days prefer to control numbers by 'lamping.'

This involves going out at night with a rifle and a very bright light. A fox, being naturally curious, will stand and stare at the approaching lamp, giving a marksman a chance to shoot it. Shooting is, of course, often the urban dweller's only concession to culling, but as countryman R. W. F. Poole observed, "There is a shadowy figure who in anti-hunting folklore is the definitive answer for both fox and deer control – the 'skilled marksman with a high-powered rifle.' While such people do exist, a lot of people with high-powered rifles are far from skilled and, as a result, shooting accounts for more animal suffering than most country people feel is necessary."

This little piggy went to market

Ageing animals that were originally destined for the pot or the market populate many rural smallholdings but, when the time came, the family couldn't bring themselves to do the deed.

"My father brought home a gosling with the idea that the bird would be kept and fattened for Christmas dinner. It was a wonderful little character that followed my mother around everywhere and it soon because obvious that, even if the bird were killed, noone was going to want to eat it. In the finish the grown goose was given to another family for Christmas, but their children also made such a fuss that they kept it as a pet and it eventually died of old age."

Maggie May had been acquired as a small piglet, with the idea that she would be fattened up and butchered for the freezer. Again the family knew they couldn't eat the meat if the pig was slaughtered and she went to live at Ty Agored Animal Sanctuary. She was such a popular attraction that when she came down with pneumonia Barbara Packham had to issue bulletins about the state of her health. She eventually died at the sanctuary, a long, long time after her intended life span had passed.

.....and a pony for the children

According to an article in *Horse & Hound*, buying a child's pony can be another of life's most stressful experiences, but there are a few 'tips' that can lessen the anguish if you don't know one end of a horse from the other.

- Beware of anyone who is keen to make a quick sale – a genuinely outgrown pony's owners will be very fussy about where it's going and will ask a lot of questions.

- Try to buy the pony's saddle whenever possible, because if the owner is desperate to hang on to it, it probably means they intend buying another pony the same size, and if so, why?

- Spend some time going around local Pony Club events and talk to people about ponies being moved on.

- If you haven't got a clue, take a knowledgeable person with you to try the pony.

- Don't choose a pony by appearance, or because your child sulks.

- Don't buy from a dealer.

Before agreeing to buy any horse or pony there are several important factors to be taken into account, and most of these hinge on whether you can afford to keep the animal fit and healthy. Too many animals finish up wading around in a sea of mud with no proper shelter and little in the way of food to sustain them through the winter months. Weather conditions in this country are particularly adverse to providing a healthy environment for horses' feet, which are not designed to withstand hours submerged in wet mud.

Nevertheless, there is a lot to be said for keeping horses and ponies out in winter and, according to veterinary opinion, the majority will be fitter, healthier and happier on good turn-out with a decent rug, since bringing the horses in from the cold can trigger a host of ailments.

Livery costs for an ordinary horse or pony can range from £30 to £300 per week, with you doing most of the work yourself at the cheaper end of the scale. Very often you get what you pay for, and it pays to have a look at several establishments before making up your mind. The yard should be tidy with a sense of order and provide a service well within your budget. Generally speaking, the options are as follows:

- Full livery should cover the full care of your horse, ie. stabling, feed, grooming, exercise and cleaning of tack.

- Part livery is similar to full livery, but does not include exercising and cleaning of tack.

- DIY livery means that you pay for the use of the stable and possibly grazing – but everything else you do yourself.

It is important to assess what the yard has to offer and be fully conversant as to what the service is that you are paying for – so beware of hidden extras as these can soon mount up.

One last thing to be taken into consideration before agreeing to buy a horse or pony is the annual insurance premium. Equine insurance companies have reported a record leap in the average veterinary claim over the past few years, which has affected the cost. An article in *Horse & Hound* pointed out that "while it is by no means a question of vets overcharging or cheating, thousands of pounds can easily be spent on diagnostic work without the vet ending up any the wiser as to the cause of, say lameness."

So, tempting as it may be, try to avoid acquiring livestock until you have a better idea of what you can reasonably cope with. Whether you are a country family or a city family, children will always promise faithfully to take care of the creature they've driven everyone round the bend to get.....then they lose interest and Mum usually ends up looking after it!

THE SOCIAL SCENE

Once the novelty has worn off, the countryside is more likely to be viewed as a cultural desert since there may be limited access to fashionable shops, cinemas or theatre. Again, rural folk do as they have always done, and that is to make their own entertainment, although those working on the land have little time for leisure. Getting up early in the morning to see to the animals and going to bed after the last hay has been brought in at ten or eleven o'clock at night doesn't leave much time for socialising. There are, however, several rural traditions that the incomer interferes with at their peril.

The pub

Patronage of the local hostelry is a must if we wish to become part of the village community as this rural institution usually plays host to the local sports teams, and is where the locals congregate for pre-Sunday lunch drinks. "We've got two pubs in the village," said Alexandra. "One has recently been refurbished and caters for incomers' tastes for what they think is good 'pub grub,' while the other is rough and ready where local farm workers can call in for a quick pint and a pie. Although the latter hasn't been decorated for years, it always has a roaring log fire and the food is better and at a fraction of the price. And we can pop in with the dog."

"We held our breath when new people took over the village pub," said one local. "The previous lot hadn't been what you might call obliging and the place was empty most nights. The new folk wanted a small restaurant as the wife was a chef, but they didn't sacrifice space for it and within a few weeks they'd attracted the cricket and darts team back and taken bookings for the annual club dinners. The food is good and not hellishly expensive and you need to book a table even mid-week. They've put heart back into the pub and into the community."

The Countryside Agency has estimated that more than six pubs a week are closing, while others are being turned into restaurants. Unfortunately, a refurbishment rarely retains the character of the old pub and locals aren't welcome in their boots and work clothes, and neither are the dogs. Village pubs, like The Woolpack in Emmerdale, should remain the focal point for socialising for everyone, but locals

71

and incomers are rarely united in what they think makes for a good village pub.

The church

This is still the heart of many villages and not because the community is particularly religious. In many instances the church plays host to the mothers' union, the youth club, baby and toddler groups, the harvest supper and lunch or supper clubs for the elderly in the parish, as well as organising numerous fund raising events for various local causes. Very often the people supporting these events, either by donating or buying, are rarely ever seen in the pews for Sunday service.

One couple were quite pleased about the way they'd given the vicar short shrift when he'd called just after they'd moved in. "We soon told him where to get off," said the husband. "We don't go in for any of that religious nonsense." As a result they were never invited to anything and were soon heard complaining that they were left out of things happening in the village.

By contrast, another incomer explained that although there was a difference of religious opinion (she was a Buddhist), she was nevertheless always willing to support his community activities. "The parish newsletter was always pushed through the door and we gave to the various projects he got up to raise funds for the church. We even attended the carol service one year and his face was a joy to see when we walked in. He never tried to push the religious question and often dropped in for coffee and a chat."

Rural vicars don't tend to be as thorny as their more urban colleagues, simply because it doesn't pay. The fly-on-the-wall television documentary about the 'protesting vicar' merely showed a man out of his depth in a country environment, and in the end he lost heart and resigned. Country parsons (as they used to be called) are a very special breed, and it may be a mistake to dismiss them out of hand just because you don't share their particular faith.

The village hall

Every country person has fond memories of the village hall because at one time every activity in the area was focussed on these peculiarly rural British institutions. This is where we came for the Saturday night dance, the baby welfare clinic and it also served as a meeting place for the local Cubs, Brownies, Guides and Scout troops. They provided the venue for family parties and wedding receptions, the local amateur dramatic society performed the annual pantomime there and the youth club catered for sulky teenage girls who only went along for the records and the boys, not to learn macramé or play ping-pong.

"Our village hall was quite primitive, but it provided us with a venue for a weekly dance," says Sue. "To give it a bit of atmosphere, the organisers would swop all the normal light bulbs for red and blue ones, and the source of the music was an ordinary record-player, with everyone bringing the latest from their own personal collections. The hall consisted of one large room with a stage, two toilets and a back kitchen that often had stinging nettles growing through the floor. Oh, the good old days!"

Unfortunately, with the shift in local facilities and entertainment, village halls have been in decline for years, with no local funding available for repairs and modernisation. As a result, most are musty, hard to clean, almost impossible to heat and incredibly barracks-like in appearance, but they still represent the social heart of many rural communities.

The village school

Those who went to village schools often received a broader education than many of their urban contemporaries, despite there only being a couple of teachers trying to cater for forty or so pupils of all different ages. As well as the normal schooling there were practical nature walks, the school band and choir, basic French, beekeeping, country dancing, the annual sports day and participation in the local fete. The pupils came from all social backgrounds and the teaching disciplines set the classless structure for village life, where the offspring from the 'big house' grew up to play cricket and hunt with the children of the local butcher. Few 'wealthy' children went to private school until they reached eleven years of age.

Unfortunately, many of these village schools have closed and as a result, the community spirit is no longer nurtured in the classroom, simply because children often have to travel miles by bus for schooling, or are dropped at the gates by the 'milk-run' mums. It means that children form friendships with others who live much further afield rather than those from the same village.

"Although my friend Hilary and I had completely different family interests, we lived in the same village and were inseparable for the first 15 years of our lives," said Sue. "She stayed behind in the village and worked locally, while I went off to London. We're now in our 60s, but we regularly keep in touch even though we now have very little in common apart from those roots, but they go very, very deep."

Many village schools have been sold for conversion to private homes, but those that do remain open still offer a community meeting place for those who live in the area. "The heart went out of the place when they closed the school," said one farmer whose yard is situated in the middle of the village next to the school yard. "The whole village felt as if it had died when the children's voices weren't heard in the playground any more."

Which is why there is always a strong campaign against the closure of a village school, and you'll win quite a few brownie points if you support the protest, even if you don't have children living with you.

The Women's Institute

Never underestimate the power of the local Women's Institute – after all, these are the ladies who dealt Tony Blair such a well-mannered blow when he tried to inveigle them in his politics. This well-publicised event demonstrated to the world at large that the WI wasn't just about ladies in twin-sets and pearls arranging flowers and making jam.

The first WI was founded in 1897 from the ideas of Adelaide Hoodless so that women could enjoy similar educational and social advantages to those given to the men at the Farmers' Institute. The original WIs were based exclusively in rural areas and through close community ties and wide ranging activities, the organisation has played a unique role. With a current membership of around 220,000, the National Federation of Women's Institutes is an educational, social, non-political and non-sectarian organisation that offers local women the opportunity for learning, campaigning and friendship – and not just in the traditional interests such as arts and crafts, but also in the latest developments in IT, health, fitness and science.

For women moving into a rural area, the WI does offer the opportunity to play an active part in the community and make friends through social, practical and leisure activities. Prior experience of committee work, fund raising, public speaking and social issues can lead to new members eventually taking a more effective part in community life without the aggravation often directed at newcomers in more 'localised' groups.

During its long history, the WI has also undertaken a large number of valuable localised publishing ventures, which have preserved regional history, recipes and folk customs for posterity. Catering for the growing interest in local history, there probably isn't a rural Post Office in the country that doesn't sport a collection of illustrated guides to various towns and villages or postcards of historical buildings in the parish, many sponsored by the WI.....and then, of course, there was that calendar.

The County Show

County Shows and Game Fairs attract people of all persuasions, for this is where they can meet sympathetic folk with communal interests and expertise. The County Shows are much more of a tourist attraction, but they provide a great day out with something for everyone. They are often one of the highlights of the farmers' calendar where they can indulge themselves in the pleasures of the stock ring without the mucking out.....and have a little tipple in the beer tent. They can inspect agricultural machinery they can't afford.....and have a little tipple on the trade stand.

There is all sorts of local produce to sample, including local cheeses, sausages, home-made pies and pickles, with the 'Best of Show' often destined for the local butcher's slab come Christmas. "That was a problem," says Lewis. "Our local butcher used to have a photograph on show of some magnificent beast, complete with rosettes and full pedigree and tell us that this was to be our Christmas dinner! Keeping and showing sheep ourselves has made us less sentimental, but we still feel uncomfortable if the animal was known to us."

Despite the predominantly agricultural slant, the really big shows like the Bath & West, Royal Welsh, Royal Highland, the Royal Show and the Three Counties provide a most enjoyable day out for all the family. And even the more localised events still offer the opportunity to rub shoulders with local people in a party atmosphere that even the most persistent rain can't dampen.

Cheap holidays and Bank Holiday weekends

"We moved into our country cottage a month away from Easter and by the second week we'd already got guests booked in for the long weekend, and had a blazing row with my brother because someone else had got in first," remembers Alex. "From then, right up until the August Bank Holiday, nearly every weekend was taken up entertaining visitors."

This is a fact of life when moving to the country and every visitor will want to do the sights – which may be fine for the first few occasions, but the novelty soon wears off. "If I never see St. Fagan's again (the Welsh Open Air Folk Museum) it won't be too soon for me," said one incomer to the Principality. "It really is the most amazing place, but every one of our visitors in the first year wanted to see it, even those who'd been warned that it was a full day out with lots of walking. By the second year my husband's eyes glazed over at the mere mention of the place."

Entertaining non-stop guests can be an extremely expensive and tiring business, especially if there is livestock to look after. If you want to retain your sanity, ear-mark certain 'no-go' areas in your diary when it won't be convenient for folk to visit. After a little bit of practice, "Oh, I'm sorry, we're busy that weekend," will trip lightly off your tongue. Even the dearest of friends and family will start to treat you like a convenient B&B (without the luxury of payment) for regular weekends away, so steel yourself before they begin to take advantage.

Go on a treasure hunt

When we talk about 'treasure' we're referring to the various goodies that can be bought locally and which are often produced on our doorstep, without us knowing anything about it. One couple tracked down a grower of those incomparable Pembroke potatoes, and discovered a veritable 'farm shop' of local produce at a fraction of supermarket cost.

A Hereford farming family, having grown their own potatoes for years, diversified by producing their own crisps on the farm and now it's not unusual for a potato to be dug in the morning and made into crisps by lunchtime! "Unlike most commercial crisp makers who use brokers to source their potatoes and mass produce their crisps in factories, we're in control from seed to crisp," says a spokesman for Tyrells. "Our own direct distribution to independent retailers throughout the UK ensures total freshness of our crisps, seasonal additions and hand-fried vegetables."

Barbara Fredriksson and Nicola Dent created an organic herb farm and were soon growing 200 varieties of flowers and herbs and supplying them to local garden centres. Their business really took off when, after a long cold day in a muddy field, the prospect of a long soak in a hot bath germinated the idea of producing an exotic range of traditional cold-processed soaps. Production begins with the harvesting of the farm's organically grown herbs in June and July for drying purposes. Using only natural ingredients, within a very short time The Celtic Herbal Company was supplying garden centres, top London stores, historic Welsh castles and beauty salons.

These treasure troves mean that many of those living and working in the country only use the supermarkets for what shopkeepers in our parents' day would have referred to as 'dried goods' – tinned and packeted foods, toiletries and cleaning items.

Car boot sales

Rural car boot sales are always much more interesting that urban affairs simply because many of the latter are attended by a large number of seasoned market traders, and do not offer the variety and bargains. In the countryside nearly everyone goes to the Sunday morning 'boot,' if only to stock up on fresh vegetables for the coming week.

Normally, a farmer will set aside a field and allow the weekly 'boot' to be held on his land from around Easter to September. Often these events have replaced the weekly market that would have been held in the surrounding small towns and villages, so the whole affair has a 'market-day' feel to it, and is more of a social occasion than those run in the larger towns.

"Country people have always worked on the principle that one person's rubbish is another's bargain," said one regular 'booter.' "I've curtained the whole house since we moved here for a fraction of the cost, and we're not talking rubbish either."

"I've equipped my tool shed with really good, old fashioned tools," said another. "There's a chap who specialised in cleaning and renovating craftsman's tools and he polishes them up until the brass fittings shine again. I get a great deal of pleasure out of owning and using them, and if anything needs sharpening I bring it over for him to do."

Most spring and summer Sunday mornings produce a regular flow of adults, children and dogs, who all come along just to wander around, pick up the odd bargain, or enjoy a hot roast pork roll with a coffee while their partners do the browsing.

Farmers' markets

More and more people want to know where their food comes from, as is shown by the growing popularity of farmers' markets and the spread of more detailed labelling in family butchers. In fact, in the past few years, farmers' markets have become an established feature in old market squares, halls and high streets throughout the country. The National Association of Farmers' Markets have compiled a directory of all registered farmers' markets across the country and if there's one near you, go along and see what's on offer.

One food writer weekends at the family's cottage in Dorset where her husband runs a shoot. "I wouldn't have a real understanding of food, the thing I work with, if I didn't mix with the farmers. One of my best friends is the dairy farmer and I get all my meat down there, and game."

Local farmers' markets are advertised in most local papers and, although many are still held monthly, more and more are now being held weekly, and the choice of produce is expanding all the time. There are now wide selections of garden plants on sale and these are springing up alongside the stalls selling beef, farmhouse cheese, home-made pickles and organic fruit and vegetables.

The stalls are usually open from 10.00am-12.00 noon and the more productive markets have moved into church/village halls so that visitors can have somewhere to have a coffee and a chat. As one new customer quickly found out, "You'll find people doing their weekly shop there because the food is much fresher than any supermarket can offer."

We need to remember that supposedly 'fresh' supermarket food has often been shipped around the world, either in chilled storage containers or sealed in inert gas bags to slow down the rotting process. Some 'fresh' food can actually be more than six months old.

People are finding that they prefer the taste of fresh food – sprouts from a farmers' market that may have been picked earlier in the morning, for example. As a result, the markets are becoming a normal part of shopping rather than something unusual.

COUNTRY PURSUITS AND PASTIMES

Rural people don't have a lot of superfluous time for socialising, simply because they are too busy working on the land or, if they do take time off, it is usually spent hunting, shooting or fishing – or some other allied pastime. Leisure is strongly linked to the 'day job' and unless you have an interest in learning more about country pursuits, here's where the dividing line between town and country is at its broadest.

By and large countrymen are by nature a hardy bunch who can endure the harshest of conditions in pursuit of their chosen sport. They work hard and play hard, often sustaining the most appalling injuries while going about their business. Rural wives get used to having their man brought home in the back of a Land Rover, battered, bruised, broken and covered in mud after a skirmish on the hunting or rugby field. In the country this is all part of life's rich tapestry, and so is appearing in the pub the next day, battered, bruised and broken, but minus the mud.

Action men are the first to laugh at themselves and the painful predicaments they find themselves in and, by and large, have extremely high pain thresholds, which any incomer would be hard pressed to match. So, if contemplating taking up any rural action man pursuits, don't expect any sympathy in times of injury – just learn to grin and bear it.

The cricket club

One pastime where you would not be expected to risk life and limb is village cricket, which is a long way removed from the commercial politics and pastel jump-suits of the Oval. In fact, as Tim Head observed, in village cricket the game still survives in a form that would be recognisable to W. G. Grace and his brothers. "And is there still honey for tea?" Well yes, actually, and it's a good strong sweet brew from the same huge tin or enamel teapots they'd have used 100 years ago, or even earlier.

Of all the rural traditions village cricket is the one that can still attract budding youngsters who may not find a place in the school team, a veritable army of tea-ladies, muscular farm workers and vicars in mufti.

The cricket pitch is usually an immaculately kept rectangle of green in the middle of a cow pasture, and those in the position of 'fielders' spend a considerable amount of time rummaging around to retrieve the ball from cowpats.

But the village cricket season offers more than just a way of spending a pleasant afternoon lolling about in a deck chair and listening to the sound of leather on willow. The teams are often desperately short of players, particularly around the time of hay making and harvest, and incomers who casually volunteer to 'make up the numbers if you need me' will quickly be absorbed into village life. Don't be offended if you're dropped the following week because a 'local' is back in the slips.....just turn up and support them anyway.

The beauty of village cricket is that you don't have to be good at it, although it helps. One recently arrived fellow was watching a game and suddenly found himself enlisted for the following weekend, despite the fact that he hadn't held a cricket ball since he was at school. "A few games into the season and we'd been invited to all sorts of cricket 'dos' which we wouldn't have known anything about if I hadn't agreed to play. It doesn't matter if you're 'out' with the first ball, you're part of the team and no one cares, but it is the best way to get to know people, although my wife has yet to agree to help with the teas."

The supporters of the annual cricket club dinner and dance are often those who participate in all sorts of other local activities, and so this is an area to be explored by all members of the family.

Keeping an eye on the ball

Rugby and football have a keen following in the country, and are more than likely to have the supporters' club based in the village pub. Local leagues are taken very seriously indeed, but forget about the neatnesses of urban clubs and municipal pitches. In the country the pitch is the corner of some windswept field and, apart from the players and a handful of die-hard supporters, the only other spectators will be a herd of cows and a bored dog, all of whom will invade the pitch just as the local striker is about to score.

By half-time the pitch will resemble the Somme as the teams, by now completely indistinguishable from each other, wallow hock-deep in mud. Some clubs have their own clubhouse complete with bath, but in most cases the end of the game is heralded by a wide assortment of hairy bottoms and jock-straps being exposed in the car park. This is rural sport at its finest and wives who have any sense simply leave them to it. Show too much interest and you could be the one putting umpteen sets of mud caked kit through your washing machine.

You have been warned!

The huntin,' shootin' and fishin' brigade

Whether we like it or not, hunting, shooting and fishing are an integral part of country life and often provide the only social activities available in rural areas. Enough has been said and written on the subject of hunting, but suffice to say that this has been a traditional part of the British countryside for hundreds of years. Regardless of which side of the debate we decide to take, it can only be stressed that it is a subject upon which opinion should not be over-ridden by either sentiment or ignorance of country ways.

One often overlooked aspect that is becoming increasingly popular among all walks of life is ferreting, the basics of which haven't changed a lot since it started in medieval times. The ferret is used to flush rabbits out from their underground warrens to be caught by whichever means the hunter chooses, which may be shooting, using nets, a dog, a hawk or any number of combinations.

Rob had kept ferrets for many years before moving them to the country. "I often take the ferrets to a farmer whose land is over-run with rabbits and we can bag quite a high number. Here my enthusiasm is accepted, whereas when I lived in a town I was considered a bit odd for keeping them. And what I heard is true. Wild rabbit does taste better than farmed ones!"

Although not every one can afford to belong to an organised pheasant shoot, farmers and gamekeepers periodically issue an invitation to local shooting enthusiasts to 'man the coverts and flight woodpigeons' on a Saturday afternoon to help with the pest control. Our large population of woodpigeons is mainly resident, but some migrate to north-west Europe and migrants arrive in Britain during October and November to leave in March and April. A flock of pigeons can cause considerable damage on agricultural land as a single pigeon eats a handful of grain or seedlings a day, so a flock of 1,000 birds can strip acres of arable land in no time at all.

Despite the large flocks woodpigeons are not easy targets, especially as when flying with a strong wind behind them they can be exceeding some sixty miles per hour! As any pigeon shooter will explain, it is a much more exciting sport that other feathered game. Pigeons are canny and it takes hours of reconnaissance to reap rewards. It is also a sport in which every bird taken is eaten, either by the shooters themselves or via a local game dealer.

Before taking the moral high ground on any aspect of field sports we should remember that of the 270,000 wild animals and birds slaughtered on the roads each year, the majority are killed by non-sporting people. Many aren't killed outright and are left to die an agonising death unless a passing sportsman stops and puts them out of their misery.

The village fete

An appearance at the annual church or village fete is a must, even if the thought of weak tea and warm beer is the last thing you need on a summer Saturday afternoon. Most villages still have coloured bunting that was used to celebrate the Coronation and the marquee will have seen better days at the Scout camp, but don't be deceived into thinking this is purely a quaint local affair. This is an important annual fund raising event and even if you don't attend church, it is a worthwhile cause to support in terms of community good will.

The number of stalls and events may not be as varied as they once were when village fetes were held in the gardens of large country houses. Nowadays they are more than likely confined to the school playground or the 'rec' (recreation field), and finding people to support the event dwindles every year, with incomers often outnumbering locals. Nevertheless, the fete still stumps up the traditional assortment of arts and crafts, the cake and bottle stalls, tombola and 'find the treasure' or guess how many beans/marbles are contained within a large glass jar.

There's no traditional 'bowling for the pig' any more, although one local organiser kept the spirit of the game alive by offering an assortment of china and fluffy pigs as prizes and in another village the butcher donated half a pig for the freezer. Wellie throwing has always been a popular event, but perhaps the best of all is the white elephant stall, where all the unwanted odds and sods from the village are recycled year after year. The local school often takes part by providing displays of fancy dress, face painting, country dancing and the (let's be honest!) excruciating school band that bangs and wheezes its way through traditional folk tunes like Greensleeves!

Pony and/or donkey rides expect the poor beasts to trek aimlessly backwards and forwards carting toddlers, who are held in the saddle by a nervous parent. "My dog disgraced itself at one fete," admits one embarrassed owner. "He'd never seen a donkey before and curiosity got the better of him. As the animal passed he stuck a cold nose in its nether regions and it took off, bucking like something out of a Thelwell cartoon with both parent and handler hanging on to the passenger, who had a good twelve inches of daylight between her bottom and the saddle. Noone noticed what had set the poor donkey off, so we slunk away to the other end of the playing field before our guilty expressions gave us away."

There are 'brownie points' to be gained for volunteering to man a stall or helping in the tea tent, so keep an eye open for the tell-tale signs. In the good old days the village fete was followed by a dance in the village hall in the evening, but this has been replaced by a barbecue or a hog roast and disco.

The Game Fair

Unlike the County Shows the local Game Fair offers very little by way of a sop to tourism, being the province of traditional hunters, shooters and fishermen. This arcane world is where real country folk go to relax and if anyone doubts the popularity of field sports, they should make the effort to visit a CLA Game Fair. This is the UK's largest country sporting event and is always held in a beautiful setting, with shooting, fishing, gundogs, gamekeeping and falconry remaining the core elements of the show.

On a more local level the fair will be a one or two day affair somewhere between a County Show and village fete and often a lot more fun. "The mink hounds were billed as putting in an appearance," said one local. "The wagon backed into the area, the huntsmen turned out in royal blue with red gaiters, blew the horn and the hounds tumbled out on to the grass. That was the last we saw of them. They picked up a scent and hurtled out of the arena, out of the showground and disappeared completely. There was a lot of yelling and horn-blowing, but we never saw them again!"

Game fairs offer more of an opportunity to get closer and spend time with those who know more about country living than the sales personnel that man the trade stands at the County Shows. There are falconry displays (and the birds often clear off, too!) and ferret, lurcher and terrier racing where the family pet can enter for the princely sum of 50p, not to mention equestrian events for all levels and ages.

More than one memory has been triggered by Game Fairs. "In the main arena one of the attractions was a chap who was simulating all the old poachers' tricks for the entertainment of the crowd. His display was cleverly contrived by using a series of elastic lures to make the fake 'rabbits' streak across the field into the long-net. It was so convincing that two visiting whippets joined in the fun, much to the delight of the crowd and the embarrassment of their owner.

"I'd been watching the display and re-living my own memories of poaching which had been long forgotten," said Sue. "A long-net was some two foot high and some 20 feet long and held upright by cut hazel sticks.....how did I know they were hazel sticks? Because it had been my job to carry them. The story goes back to my pre-school years and my father left baby sitting for reasons I can't remember. He'd done the 1939-45 stint in North Africa and Europe and it took a long, long time to get the adrenalin buzz out of his system. Being a countryman he turned his hand to a spot of DIY recreational therapy (ie. poaching) because that was the way you coped in those pre-counselling days. It was a fine night with a poacher's moon; myself (aged about four) and the dog (about the same age) were bundled on to the motorbike and off we went into the darkness of the woods for a few hours of illicit hunting.

"This happened several times until my mother found out – then there was all hell to pay and these night-time excursions were stopped. Today, social services would consider leaving a four-year old alone in the dark holding a poacher's net an act of extreme neglect, if not cruelty. For me it represents wonderful memories. It also means that I have no fear of being alone in remote places during the hours of darkness – which was just as well now living in Wales and roaming about the fields at midnight with the dog, star watching."

For sheer entertainment for the whole family, the local Game Fair is an event not to be missed and who knows, you might just learn something.

The answer's a horse

It must be obvious by now that a considerable amount of country socialising revolves around horses, and that hunting forms an integral part of those equestrian pursuits. As Serena Soames points out, "The Pony Club is an institution that fosters independence and confidence in children. It grew out of the hunting umbrella, so that children should learn to ride well enough to be able to ride to hounds. The hunting field is used to refresh stale competition horses; it is a training ground for point-to-pointers and steeplechasers; it is a nursery for most of the steeplechase jockeys riding in Britain and provides a second career for competition horses that have peaked."

Also organised by local hunts, another of the most challenging of equine sports is team-chasing, which is almost as thrilling for spectators as it is for the participants. Team-chasing as a recognised sport is less than 30 years old, but considered to be one of the equestrian world's most exhilarating pastimes. Anyone can take part, but it is impossible to overlook the very obvious ties to foxhunting (ban or no ban), since most of the riders and spectators will be members or followers of the local hunt.

This is a race against the clock with the times of the first three in the team counting (the sport's name coming from the idea that each team has a leader who sets the pace); the last member home is untimed. The event has been modified from the original 'natural' obstacles, but the ride is still not for the faint-hearted. A Daily Telegraph Weekend report observed that "Team-chasing is a sport for those who abhor the nanny state. Few back protectors are in sight (compulsory in eventing), while there are no barriers or ropes behind which the spectators must stand." As an extension of the hunting scene, the social aspect of team-chasing is as important as the actual participation, and the teams usually ride under such incongruous names as Feisty Fillies, Stroppy Mares and Three Old Farts and a Tart. Here there's no battle of the sexes, since both are more than adept at trading the most colourful of insults, but unlike urban sportspeople, no one takes offence.

Should any member of the family discover an aptitude for horsemanship, rest assured it won't be long before the prickly subject of hunting is raised at the breakfast table. "Josie suddenly announced that she'd been invited to go hunting with one of her school friends, whose entire family regularly took part. All hell broke loose. Siblings were screaming at each other and we (as parents) tried to explain that it was cruel, but Josie was adamant that she was going. For weeks none of the girls were speaking to each other, but she stuck it out and went along. We were hoping that she would find the whole thing totally abhorrent but she didn't; she loved it and that's the set she mixes with now. It's something we don't discuss."

A large number of social events in rural areas are arranged by the hunt members and can range from muddy treasure hunts to highly sophisticated dinners and include people from all walks of life. In the country the horse is still king and it's the equestrian events that draw the dividing line between those from the country and those of the country.

Point-to-point

Point-to-point racing is another of those peculiarly rural activities that, up until recently, offered little attraction for those not born and bred to standing about in muddy fields for hours on end in the cold and wet. In more recent years, however, point-to-point has been attracting a much wider audience despite the spor's hunting associations, simply because it offers a chance to watch highly competitive racing fixtures.

Run by enthusiastic amateurs as fund raisers, even the most experienced of riders can find themselves volunteering for the job of car park attendant, race-card seller, timekeeper, announcer, commentator, steward or, the most thankless task of all, judge. The races are run under strict rules and competitors must hold a Rider's Qualification Certificate issued by the Jockey Club, and are only eligible if they are members of a hunt.

All horses running in point-to-points need to have been registered at birth by Wetherbys', and to hold a passport showing details of their birth and parentage. In addition, the horse has to be 'regularly and fairly hunted,' after which the Master will sign and issue a Hunter Certificate.

Originally run straight across country (hence the name), these races are now conducted on official tracks with built-in fences, usually on farmland belonging to a member of the hunt. There are about 120 courses throughout the British Isles with the form and results being closely followed by the supporters. This is a day for stocking up the 4x4 with plenty of warming food and drink and going with the intention of placing a few bob on who you think will be the winner.

Fornication

If you're a life long fan of Jilly Cooper then it may come as a disappointment to find that Rutshire is fictitious! Having said that, the rural attitude to sexual matters in general has a much more casual approach. Remember that from a very early age, country children are continuously up against birds and animals doing what comes naturally, which can lead to some embarrassing moments. "I can remember coming home from the farm, aged about eight, and much to my mother's mortification, describing in graphic detail the process of bovine artificial insemination to a rather prudish maiden aunt who happened to be visiting," says Sue.

"Alison was looking for a rich farmer to keep her and her horses, but she reckoned without the lusty appetite of the countryman," laughed Jayne. "Our local hunting crowd is notorious for its cavalier attitude to sex and she was most offended that several of the more eligible chaps had got their leg over and quickly moved on to a more challenging quarry. She really believed that her girlie good looks and fluttering eyelashes were going to get her the pick of the bunch, but the farmers are a canny lot around here."

Rosemary, on the other hand, took up dressage after her marriage broke down and it wasn't too long before she and her instructor found they had a lot in common. After a brief romance they married and she now helps him to run the equine business. "I wasn't looking for another partner, and neither was he," she said. "It was a relationship that grew out of a mutual interest and friendship."

Single ladies be warned, however; romance and foreplay isn't high on the list of priorities of the countryman, so don't expect many compliments or flattery. "The tell-tale signs that a countryman finds a woman attractive is a casual remark to a friend that she is a 'fine-looking woman,' or that she's 'well turned-out'," says Jayne. "If he happens to be married and his wife overhears the comment, sit back and watch the action!"

Politics & the Parish Council

Village life is ruled by the politics of the parish council and nothing will infuriate the locals more than an incomer standing for election when they've only been in the village for five minutes. The intrigues and covert operations that are brought into play are reminiscent of an episode of *Yes, Minister!* as they plot and scheme to thwart the ambitions of the interloper.

Villagers will be forced to put themselves up for election, even though they hadn't particularly wanted to (and probably don't have the time), but any move will be considered justified on the grounds that "We don't want strangers saying what should and what shouldn't be done in the village when they've only just moved in." And the 'only just moved in' status can last for ten years or more, depending on how well the family integrates into village life.

If you feel the urge to join the parish council and don't mind disclosing the most intimate of your financial assets for the scrutiny of every Tom, Dick and Harriet, then wait about five years before offering – and another ten before everyone supports you.

A demonstration of how a difference in perspective can inflame a community followed the annual 'burning an effigy' at the local bonfire night. Every year, in one particular village, the organisers decide on an effigy of someone who has particularly annoyed the villagers during the previous 12 months. Once it was a television celebrity, another time it was a local land agent, but one year it was a group of travellers who had left a dreadful mess in one of the fields just outside the village. Unfortunately, a newcomer took exception and the next thing the villagers knew, several had been arrested on charges of racism against gypsies.

The organisers claimed there was no racist intent, simply because the travellers in question were not gypsies. Another villager, whose work with gypsies was widely known locally, commented, "If I left a lot of rubbish around and they burned my effigy, I would just accept it. Some people don't see the carnival innocence in these rituals." However, mention the newcomer's name in the village now and people go quiet, and while the general consensus of opinion is that the effigy was ill-considered, there is more resentment directed towards the person who caused the trouble. "They seems to think they can tell us what to do when they've only been here five minutes," said one.

Needless to say, the newcomers in question don't go out much these days as the unwelcome, stony silence of the villagers doesn't look as if it is likely to go away. Local politics can be a minefield for the unwary, so it is best avoided unless you have the hide of a rhinoceros.

BACK TO NATURE

Until the Second World War, farming in Britain had changed very little. England and Wales were still largely a patchwork of mixed farms with small fields or sheep grazing on the uplands. When the crops were harvested, the stubble was left in the soil until it was ploughed for the next sowing in the spring. The thin soil of the chalk downlands was never ploughed and neither were the water meadows. The agricultural revolution of the 1950s changed all that and, as a result, many of the wild flowers and birds that thrived on the downs and in the meadows around the villages were destroyed.

At the Countryside Restoration Trust's Lark Rise Farm, much of this balance has been restored – not with government support but by using common sense. Not only has the wildlife returned, but this is farmed land where the tenant farmer actually makes a profit. The idea for the CRT was first mooted many years ago when the imminent destruction of the countryside had become almost a certainty.

"We decided to start an organisation that would buy intensively farmed land and work it sustainably to encourage wildlife back, while providing high-quality, safe, humanely produced food," says country journalist Robin Page. Since those days the priorities have changed slightly, because the farmer and the farm worker are now as endangered as the wildlife, "so we want to keep people on the land too, thus creating a balanced, living, working countryside."

The growth of the farm has been astonishing and Lark Rise Farm is now nearly 360 acres. Its successes have been achieved by exploiting existing agri-environmental schemes. "We have, for instance, employed a jigsaw of aids under the Countryside Stewardship Scheme and the Arable Stewardship Scheme, enabling us to criss-cross Lark Rise Farm with a network of grass margins around cereal fields."

The CRT has since bought the historic Turnastone Court Farm whose hay meadows and pasture had not been ploughed for more than 400 years. In addition, it has been given more land; a beautiful south-facing 32 acre bluebell wood in Yorkshire, in the heart of *Last of the Summer Wine* country and an astonishing livestock farm in Hereford. Not only does Awnells Farm demonstrate how to run a livestock farm in an environmentally friendly way, it also has an ancient orchard containing old strains of perry pears and cider apples. The CRT hopes to use this as a demonstration farm for those interested in preserving the traditional English farmscape.

Many conservationist groups would have the public believe that they are the only ones capable of preserving and 'governing' the landscape for posterity, but in reality it's the farmer who is the true custodian of the countryside, and who really understands Nature.

If it's got fur or feathers—it bites (again)

Or at least something that lives on it does, as a neighbour found out to his cost when he and his wife 'rescued' a small fox cub from the roadside verge. They phoned the local RSPCA, who told them to put it back where they found it. The cub was duly returned, together with a blanket, a hot water bottle and a large plate of dog food! When they returned an hour later the cub's mother had obviously retrieved it and all was well.....until the couple got home and found that their bodies were a mass of red flea bites, and the dogs were scratching themselves silly. Baby Reynard had left them a rather unwelcome thank you present.

Hedgehogs also carry an impressive amount of personal livestock, despite the Mrs. Tiggywinkle persona, so beware of picking one up. Hedgehog fleas are different from cat and dog fleas, but fleas from one species can transfer to another on a temporary basis, as many dogs will testify, although members of the medical profession may tell you otherwise!

Bats often find themselves grounded in daylight hours, having been attacked by a cat. Again, these tiny creatures will bite when frightened and, as they can carry rabies, are best left to specialists to handle. Remember that bats are a protected species and even if they invade your home you are not allowed to remove or disturb them. If it does become necessary to move one for its own safety, make sure you're wearing a stout pair of gardening gloves.

Recently a rural community found itself subjected to regular buzzard attacks because the footpath to a new housing development took pedestrians and cyclists too close to where the birds were nesting. There were lots of protests but again the buzzard is protected, and in any case, was only protecting its young.

Wild animals have no concept of being 'rescued' as one hunt saboteur discovered and was most indignant because the fox he'd pounced on to 'save,' turned around and bit him quite badly in the face. To the fox his behaviour was seen as threatening and the animal reacted accordingly. Wild animals do not stop to rationalise whether we mean them harm or not and are best left to their own devices, unless their situation is life-threatening.

What you can and can't do:

Rabbits: As long as you do not set out to cause deliberate suffering you do not need permission to kill rabbits and there is no limit to the number you can kill. In fact, under regulations dating from 1952 you are obliged to control rabbits on your land, although this does not mean completely eradicating them.

Mink: Mink farming was banned on the supposition that it is cruel to farm animals for their skin alone and those in the wild today are the descendents of escapees, or those misguidedly released by animal activists. As the result of new legislation, mink is to be eradicated from Britain and landowners are encouraged to kill or trap them; it is illegal to release them once caught. Trapping mink, however, is a hazardous business because a) the animals are extremely vicious and b) they tend to share their environment with highly protected otters and polecats.

Moles: Despite its cute *Wind in the Willows* reputation, no other animal causes as much devastation to gardens and pastureland as the mole. You rarely get to see one, but you will certainly notice the mess they leave behind. Farmers who make a lot of silage cannot risk soil contamination of the cut grass (which can cause listeriosis in sheep), and so they are keen to keep mole populations to a minimum on their land. Spring traps are designed to kill moles and are exempt from legislation, with no permission required to use them.

Badgers: No longer rare, but it is illegal to disturb their setts in any way under pain of a £5,000 fine or six months in jail for every animal killed. Badger setts are recognisable by the evidence of paw prints, hair, grass and hay outside, but no droppings which they bury in pits.

Grey squirrels: Still regarded as an alien species that must be killed if caught as they are responsible for the decimation of the native red squirrel population and for killing young trees and saplings. If you unintentionally catch one in a trap you will be breaking the law if you let it go!

Goshawks: Although they are prolific killing machines capable of devastating free range chicken farms, the law treats them like an endangered species - which they are not.

The rest: The so-called 'Section Six' animals which cannot be harmed or disturbed without permission from DEFRA are bats, wildcats, dormice, hedgehogs, pine martens, common otters, polecats, shrews and the red squirrel. If any of these animals were accidentally caught in a trap you would be breaking the law if you did not return them at once to the wild.

Rats: It is said that wherever we live we are never less than a few feet from a rat and, for most people, this creature produces the greatest fear after snakes. Rats were one of the few pests that private homeowners could have disposed of at public expense, although the fact that local authorities now charge for pest control is believed to account for the dramatic increase in the rat population. Homeowners are free to dispose of them however they wish, so long as no undue suffering is caused - such as 'catching them by the feet'!

Two species of rat occur in the British Isles; the brown or common rat and the black rat. The latter was introduced during the 11th or 12th century, and for 600 years was the common rat of the British countryside, having arrived in the baggage of the crusaders. The more versatile brown rat was introduced in the late 1720s and by the 20th century the black rat had almost disappeared.

Although mainly associated with urban areas, the brown rat also lives in open countryside in most parts of the British Isles. Many country rats make their way into farm buildings in winter and their presence can be detected by droppings or body smears produced by the greasy secretions of skin glands. Damage to food and the fabric of buildings is one reason why rats make uneasy bedfellows; another and perhaps more important reason is that they carry certain diseases, some of which are serious and even fatal to humans and domestic animals.

Rats sniff around until they find a weak spot, such as a broken air vent in a ground floor wall or the gap plumbers always leave between the outlet pipe and the washing machine where the pipe pierces the exterior brickwork. So be on your guard against these unwelcome visitors and let the dog have his bit of sport if he chases one.

Being realistic

Nature's bounty is given in many ways and country folk don't waste any of it. In fact there's an old country saying that the only thing that's wasted on a pig is its grunt. Similarly, if a local sees a pheasant hit by a passing car, he'll think nothing of stopping and picking up the casualty for his dinner. The unwritten rule is that it must be freshly killed and relatively undamaged; if it's been lying there for an hour or two, it will already have attracted other wildlife!

At one time no country kitchen was without rabbit on the menu at least once a week. Rabbits were introduced into the British Isles around the 12th century as a food source, and were originally kept in fenced enclosures. Today's wild rabbits are descended from the escapees from those former domesticated colonies, although myxomatosis, introduced in 1953, nearly wiped out the whole population, and many country folk haven't eaten wild rabbit since.

In some parts of the country it is not uncommon for deer to become road casualties, but here the unwary should think twice about visions of venison for the freezer. It may be that the carcass has lain there for some time. It may be that a vet had been called to deal with the injured animal and administered a lethal injection, the local kennels or abattoir not yet having arrived to remove the dead animal. Animals put to sleep by lethal injection cannot be fed to hounds as death would be inevitable and in such cases a vet should attach a label stating 'Do not feed.'

If the deer hasn't been killed outright, fear and pain would have increased the adrenalin pumping through its body. Ruptured intestines could have resulted in toxins being absorbed into the flesh. A spokesman for *The Countryman's Weekly* advises that risking eating venison where the cause of death is unknown could have dire consequences. "Wasteful as it may seem, if you discover a dead roadside deer it is far wiser to notify the police or a hunt kennels. The best and safest venison comes from a beast killed by a stalker's bullet."

Even town dogs quickly become accustomed to chasing squirrels and rabbits, and if they have hound or terrier blood, it won't be long before they catch one! Don't chastise the dog for doing what comes naturally and as long as the animal is dead, leave them to what can be an extremely unpleasant audible and visual episode! Polly's Rhodesian ridgeback was barely out of puppyhood when she perfected the art of rabbiting and now regularly provides her own supper. Polly just leaves her to get on with it and cuts down on the protein in her feed!

Going really green

Long hot summers with gentle rain produce a bumper crop of wild fruits in the hedgerows such as crab apples, sloes, elderberries, rosehips, hazelnuts, blackberries and rowan berries. All are delicious when made into flavoured vinegars, chutneys, jams and liqueurs, although wild fruits should be looked upon as accompaniments to meals rather than dishes in their own right. This is usually because they take a long time to pick and the amounts are relatively small. Most lack the high sugar levels of cultivated fruit, which makes them too bitter to use on their own.

Up until the Second World War most country households would have stocked up with provisions made from wild fruit. Rowan jelly is perfect with venison or game and crab apple 'cheese' gives an unusual edge to cold pork and cheddar cheese. Then there is blackberry kir and sloe gin. Try making your own horseradish from the wild variety, which is much better than any shop-bought ones. Elderberry syrup is an old Tudor remedy for winter colds, particularly when mixed with honey, hot water and a dash of whisky.

There are numerous cookery books devoted to country recipes and anyone who is seriously interested in stocking up the larder from the hedgerows should invest in one. There is nothing quite like home-made preserves and there is a certain sense of satisfaction in eating produce from the wild.

Growing it yourself

Nor is there anything quite like the satisfaction of harvesting the first crop of your own vegetables, although we can't expect to become expert gardeners overnight. As we've said earlier, much of what we grow in the garden will depend on the type of soil, and for the first few years there will be a certain amount of experimentation. For almost guaranteed results try some of the pre-grown plants from mail-order nurseries such as Samuel Dobie, who specialise in a wide variety of stock vegetables.

Be realistic about what you can grow and where. Vegetable gardening is time consuming and it might be a better idea to go for a greenhouse, patio tubs or 'raised bed' gardening to begin with. These need watering more frequently than traditional vegetable plots, but experimentation is the name of the game and if you intend to feed the family from your endeavours, container gardening is more user-friendly to begin with.

With slugs and snails forming a central part of its diet, it's not surprising that the hedgehog is looked on as the gardener's friend, and it is worth making life comfortable for Nature's unpaid pest controller. If you want to attract hedgehogs into your garden, leave wild patches of undisturbed undergrowth to provide food and shelter in the form of a 2ft square untreated wooden box for nesting and hibernation. If you have an ornamental garden pond, make sure that the hedgehogs can climb out if they fall in, as many come to grief in this way. As an added precaution, don't use slug pellets and always check any bonfires before lighting.

Slugs aren't the only problem you'll encounter in the countryside. As soon as you begin to produce a crop of succulent plants, you will immediately be visited by rabbits and, if you're really unlucky, deer!

Brer Rabbit and the vegetable patch

If you don't want to shoot the rabbits, DEFRA recommends a cage trap as the most humane method of trapping, with carrots used as bait – though their own research reveals that 4% of the animals caught in this way are injured. Be warned that it is illegal to use cage traps where young pheasants are being reared since they are more than likely to be injured in them.

Which brings us to one of those areas where town and country are always at loggerheads – the subject of culling. Although urban dwellers often see wild animals as endearing furry creatures, the reality is often more complex. Wild animals are culled (ie. the population thinned out), usually by the selective killing of the oldest and weakest – and this doesn't matter whether we are talking about deer, foxes, rooks or rabbits. A population explosion among any species will often sound the death-knell for the rest, and trapping and moving them somewhere else does not solve the problem.

Most people want to believe that by relocating the extra numbers, lives will be saved – an urban myth that has doomed countless foxes to a slow death, having been trapped in the town and released to starve in the countryside. Wild animals survive and thrive where food is plentiful; if there are areas where certain common species are few and far between, there will be a reason for it. Insufficient food, too many predators or an unsuitable habitat can all play a role, and releasing animals in poor habitats is being cruel, not kind.

Let us take an example. There isn't a very large hedgehog population in mid-Wales and we must ask ourselves why? According to wildlife writer Daniel Butler, the problem is the booming local badger population. Not only does Mr. Badger outgun the hedgehogs in the race for slugs and worms, but his powerful jaws also make short work of the hedgehog's spiny defences. By attempting to re-populate the area with hedgehogs would merely be "adding to a Welsh badger's fat reserves." Culling is a traditional pastime which took place every autumn to ensure that only the fittest animals survived the winter, rather than dying a slow, painful death from cold and starvation.

The bird table

Due to changing farming practices, urbanisation of the countryside and the swifter spread of disease, wild birds have had to adapt, becoming increasingly dependent on what we provide during the winter months. What we should not overlook is that in the spring, when the breeding season starts, the birds still need our help - but we must be careful in what we feed to them.

Avoid salty foods and snacks, whole bacon, desiccated coconut and uncooked rice as these can kill wild birds. Instead use a good quality wild bird food, starting with a peanut feeder as peanuts are a good source of oil, protein and vitamins. On the down side, peanuts are prone to developing a fungal infection that can also poison wild birds. If the nuts show signs of fungus, sprouting, have a strange smell or just look past their sell-by date, throw them out and start again.

Remember that many birds such as robins, blackbirds and thrushes are ground or table feeders and will not be tempted to use a wire basket.

Wash out birdbaths, drinking water bowls and feeders on a regular basis. Use dedicated disinfectants and wear rubber gloves as wild birds carry a variety of diseases, some of which are a danger to humans.

Since 1996 all wild birds have been protected and you will require a licence from DEFRA to control them. With some particular pests such as magpies, licences are easily granted. Poisoning, catching in nets and electrocution are prohibited. Shooting is preferred, along with a Larsen trap, which catches the bird by opening a trap door when it lands. There are still some quirky rules about what you can do with a bird once it's been trapped. For example, bullfinches can be killed or given away - but cannot be sold or bartered!

We are all being encouraged to install a selection of nesting boxes in our gardens, but often they remain there for years with only a solitary spider in residence. The reason is because the box isn't sited correctly and birds are fussy! Here are a few tips from the experts at the RSPB:

- Birds like to be sheltered from the prevailing weather and the full force of the sun. North and east-facing sites are prime locations.

- Small-holed nesting boxes for wrens and tits should be around 5ft above the ground.

- Open-fronted boxes for robins are ideal positioned among climbing plants which protect the occupants from the weather and conceal the box from magpies, cats and squirrels.

- Too many boxes will infringe on different birds' territory, although sparrows like to nest in communities.

When carrying out repairs and maintenance on buildings and gardens in the spring, do be careful about damaging nests and eggs. The RSPB urges people to delay outdoor jobs such as building repairs, pruning, tree-felling or hedge-cutting until the end of the nesting season in July and EU legislation has even gone as far as banning farmers from hedge-cutting between March and July to protect the nesting birds.

Don't pick it!

Did you know that you could be prosecuted for picking wild flowers? In fact all wild plants are given some protection under the laws of the

United Kingdom and the Republic of Ireland. Under the Wildlife & Countryside Act, 1981, which covers Britain, it is illegal to uproot any wild plant without permission from the landowner or occupier. Uproot is defined as 'to dig up or otherwise remove the plant from the land on which it is growing.' Even plants growing wild are the legal property of somebody and, for the purposes of legislation, the term 'plant' includes algae, lichens and fungi as well as true plants – mosses, liverworts and vascular plants.' Phew!

Certain rare wild plants are given legal protection against deliberate picking of the flowers, collecting, cutting, uprooting and destruction, with the regulations applying to all stages in the biological cycle of listed plants such as creeping marshwort, early gentian, fen orchid, floating water-plantain, Killarney fern, lady's slipper, marsh saxifrage, shore dock and slender naiad. Lists of rare species can be obtained from the Joint Nature Conservation Committee, or viewed on its website.

But even common plants can suffer: "On the farm we have an old bluebell wood which has been there for centuries," said one farmer's wife. "It's not an uncommon site to see newcomers walking out of there with armfuls of the flowers, which they pick without asking. No country person would ever pick bluebells because they droop as soon as they've been picked and land up in the dustbin within hours of being pulled out from the bulbs. Why the hell can't they leave them alone."

Another countrywoman remembers there being carpets of primroses in her local wood. "For years people moving into the area would come along in the spring and dig up the plants. Now, fifty years later, there are only a few areas where the primroses still flower naturally."

Beautiful but deadly

What many town people don't realise is that the British countryside has an impressive collection of highly poisonous plants and it's as well to familiarise your family with those that can have fatal results for the unsuspecting.

Ragwort is one of the most frequent causes of livestock poisoning and results in the painful death of horses, ponies and donkeys each year. The pretty yellow flower hides a poisonous heart. It can be found in a number of places, including roadsides and motorway verges, where a single plant can produce more than 1,000,000 new plants for the following season. When eaten, either fresh or in hay, ragwort causes irreversible liver damage. A woman was recently prosecuted and banned from keeping animals for life after she was found guilty of allowing two of her horses to eat the plant. Ragwort is also dangerous to humans and can cause severe blistering to the skin if handled without protective gloves.

Deadly nightshade, or to give it its more sinister name, atropa belladonna, is often found in the neighbourhood of ruins and on the sites of former gardens. The whole plant has an unpleasant smell and is generally poisonous, with the juice of the berries being especially so. These have often proved fatal to children.

There are dozens of more familiar plants such as foxgloves, daffodils and bluebells that can cause unpleasant reactions in the unsuspecting, and many more that can be fatal to cats and dogs if eaten. Invest in an illustrated book of wild flowers and make a point of studying the hedgerows near your home for the tell-tale signs of toxic plants. Unless your children are particularly precocious there is no need to dig the plants up, even if they appear in the garden; after all, many of them have been used in folk-medicine for centuries and are all part of the countryside's rich tapestry!

The British Isles also has more species of toxic fungi than anywhere else in Europe and it is not a subject that can easily be learned from books.

The external characteristics of many species are very changeable and cannot always be identified with certainty. There is nothing to beat fresh, wild mushrooms, but this is not an area for the novice because some are highly toxic and can kill. Or, as one countryman said casually over a pint, "Eat half a death cap and it's not a case of whether you may die, but how long it will take you to die."

The Good Samaritan

Hopefully the message in this chapter will come across loud and clear: a lot of harm can be caused to wild animals, birds and plant life through well-meaning interference. Unless a bird or animal is injured, leave it alone.

People who find fledglings are often tempted to interfere, but the birds are more likely to survive if left alone, because the parents are usually quite close by. Baby tawny owls, for example, often fall out of the nest, but they can quite easily climb back up the tree by using their claws as crampons. Also bear in mind that if a young bird or animal has human scent on it, the parents may abandon it, despite your good intentions.

If in doubt call any of the local wildlife organisations who can impart knowledgeable advice over the phone.

LONG WINTER NIGHTS

It's midnight in the depths of the countryside and the only sounds to be heard are the distant bleat of a sheep, the rushing of a nearby stream and the occasional hoot from an owl as it hunts along the field margin. The dog paces about nervously listening to the strange sounds made by the wind in the trees. If you or your partner are nervous of staying alone in a remote cottage miles from the nearest neighbour and with only the dog for company, then don't be tempted by the glamour of whitewashed stonewalls and the song of a skylark. By the time it comes to alter the clocks it will be a different world entirely and one that can appear hostile and threatening to those not used to isolation.

Absent friends

Having moved away from family and friends and not having made time to find new friends and interests can cause problems, especially if one of you is stuck at home alone for long periods of time. Here we find one (or both) of two common problems may arise:

- hitting the booze
- hitting the telephone

Often the only way to defeat the feeling of loneliness and isolation is to dial a friend's number. The next thing we know an hour has gone by and, if we've been supporting ourselves with a drink or two during the conversation, we could be well-oiled by the time our partner gets home. Also spare a thought for those on the receiving end of any mind-numbing conversation, and listen for the warning signs that they are becoming bored with these desperate calls for human contact. If they:

- lapse into long silences while you talk
- make periodic non-committal grunting noises
- keep trying to inject a positive note into the conversation
- frequently make excuses to get off the phone
- get a family member to say they're not in
- start leaving the answer phone on
- fail to return your calls

.....it is a fair indications that we have run out of sympathy time and that we'd better get a grip on life before our friends disappear altogether. They have lives to lead and it may not be convenient for them to spend hours on the phone merely to relieve our boredom, especially if we're slowly getting pickled on the other end.

Log fires and frozen water troughs

Not all winter days are bright sunlight and crisp frost. Mostly our days are damp and gloomy with pale skies, a heavy atmosphere and often a rawness that makes us want to stoke up the Aga and pile logs on the fire. If we don't need to go out, then the weather gives a perfectly good excuse not to, although if we have livestock depending on us for their feed and exercise, the luxury of a warm kitchen will have to wait.

It's always colder in the countryside than it is in the town, simply because the rural landscape isn't broken up by high-rise buildings and the biting winds get a clear run at the front door! "We are halfway up the valley," said one farmer's wife, "and when the westerly gales come in off the Irish Sea, there's nothing between the coast and the side of our house. Mind you, it's been standing for well over three hundred years so I guess it will last a bit longer, but during the gales you lie in bed and wait for the roof to come off, or for the chimney to come crashing down."

In the depths of a country winter all sorts of calamities can happen and the wise family should always be prepared. "One year the power lines came down and the snow was too deep for the electricity engineers to get across the fields to find the fault. The village was cut off completely for five days without light – or warmth, if you were reliant on central heating. That's why we all stick to our battered Rayburns and open fires, stock up the pantries, bring livestock close to the house and throw another dog on the bed. Quite a few new folk learned a lesson that winter, I can tell you!"

"It's haunted, you know"

Most properties that are over seventy years old will probably have played host to the Grim Reaper at some time or another, but there's nothing quite like the sounds which emanate from an old country cottage in the dark winter nights. Mention this to the woman who runs the Post Office and in no time at all you will be told that the place is haunted by old Ben, or Bob, or Walter.....

Old buildings naturally creak and groan as the building heats up or cools down, and very often weird happenings can occur because of the structure of the land on which your house is built. We know that there is a grid of underground streams and watercourses that criss-cross the entire landscape, and these may produce enough natural sound effects to convince you of your own Amityville Horror.

Dozens of homeowners are now paying considerable amounts of money to have their homes dowsed, feng shuied and cleansed in order to rid themselves of what they see as 'negative energy.' Very often those undertaking this contemporary form of exorcism arrive in an expensive car with personalised number plates and blind their clients with an arcane science relating to 'geopathic stress lines.'

What those who genuinely work with such energies will tell us is that these pockets or lines of natural energy have a habit of moving around. It's highly possible that the energy flow will be due to the natural geological environment and there's very little anyone can do to 'cure' it. So if you've just paid out a fortune to have metal rods hammered into your lawn to interrupt the negative slurry, it could have headed off in another direction by the time the cheque has been cleared by the bank.

Dowsing is an old country craft and just about anyone can do it using either two wire rods made from a metal coat-hanger or the more traditional hazel twigs. Often used in the country to locate underground springs over which to sink a well, dowsing rods (or a pendulum) will locate just about anything from underground streams and buried metal to ley lines and psychic disturbance! In fact, even in the construction industry dowsing for water or hidden cables is a 'reasonably well-known practice.'

Dr. Ted Nield of the Geological Society of London said, "There is no known scientific basis for notions of so-called 'geopathic stress.' It is a concept more akin to ley lines and natural magic than any definable force, though it is a convenient means of parting gullible people from their money. The geological environment can affect humans – and sometimes not for the good. If you live in certain areas of the country, for example, you might have to be careful about radon in unventilated spaces. Some upland peoples used to suffer from iodine deficiency as a result of their local geology. The chemistry of the water you drink leaves distinct traces in your bones. But nowadays, with modern water supplies, this natural variation is never harmful."

That's official, so make yourself a set of dowsing rods and/or a pendulum and save yourself some money.

The 'street light' debate

In one village 75% of the local people voted against street lighting, simply because the light from roads, cities, streetlamps and airports are making it impossible for most Britons to enjoy the night sky. In fact, there is so much light pollution in Britain that during the last eclipse of the moon, 80% of amateur astronomers reported that they couldn't even see our neighbouring stars in the Milky Way from their homes. Unfortunately for those campaigning to reduce light pollution, the problem has crept up so stealthily that those without a vested interest in the subject have failed to notice its scale and seriousness.

"I moved from Ireland to the Midlands to work," says one country girl, "and for me the worst thing about an urban environment is the horrible orange fog that spreads across the sky, blotting out the stars. I used to love watching the stars come out of an evening when I was at home, but here I'm lucky if I can make out the brightest ones."

Sir Martin Rees, a Cambridge professor and the Astronomer Royal, used an ornithological analogy to highlight the problem. "I don't think you have to be interested in bird watching to understand that we would all miss songbirds if they were not in our gardens. The night sky is part of our environment and we must be concerned not to degrade it, just as we are concerned not to degrade our landscape. You shouldn't have to go to a remote part of Scotland to see the stars."

One countryman, who certainly wished to remain anonymous, told his story. "For some reason best known to themselves, the local council put an awful orange light on the village bend. It was always broken because every time the council replaced the bulb, one of the lads would take his rifle and shoot it out to stop the horrible orange glare from shining into the houses opposite. It's better for everyone without it – but no one ever asked if we wanted the bloody thing in the first place!"

Space, freedom and independence.....

Unless we exercise a certain amount of personal discipline, however, all this free time can be counter-productive. Working from home is on the rise and this could be one of the prime considerations in thinking about moving to the country. All that space, freedom and independence..... time to potter in the garden, going for long, healthy walks with the dog, dropping in on friends for coffee and a leisurely lunch at the pub.

Needless to say it doesn't quite work like that, simply because it is extremely hard to draw up work/life boundaries when we work from home. And it is even more difficult to concentrate when surrounded by our personal effects because around the home there's always a job that needs doing. As a result, instead of 'working' we indulge in some displacement activity, like turning out the wardrobe or weeding the rose bed. Added to this, in farming communities there are few people about who have the time for morning coffee, or an extended pub lunch. Because we don't see anyone there is the temptation to slop around in tatty jumpers and leggings – and then we can't answer the door to a caller because we're ashamed of the way we look.

"I get up early, take the dog out and then have breakfast before reading the morning paper," says Sue, who's writing her third novel. "Then it's time to tackle the housework, with each room having a specific day for a good farm out. This takes me up to 'elevenses' and after a cup of coffee I work right through until four o'clock without a break. That gives me enough time to shower, change, get a meal ready and have the evening free. Having said all that, it took me a good two years before I could discipline myself to keep to a tight work schedule. And it wasn't easy!"

When boredom sets in

.....and it certainly will! What are you going to do when the novelty of your new home wears off, or the weather is too bad to do any gardening?

If we've moved to a remote area with limited recreational facilities, it will pay to think of some project or hobby that would keep us occupied throughout the dark afternoons and long winter evenings. Several newcomers in the village have enrolled with the Open University or taken up distance learning courses. One neighbour started her first winter by settling down to read *War & Peace*, never having had the time to even attempt it before!

On the plus side, The Daily Telegraph published a report on the positive contributions being made by incomers, in that many were creating jobs and safe-guarding local services by setting themselves up as computer consultants, accountants and freelance writers: in other words, making a significant contribution to the economy of the community. Many may have moved out of town heading for the 'good life,' but a large number have brought their entrepreneurial skills with them. Winter boredom probably gave them some breathing space to think about starting up a new venture

If we live near a medium sized town then the prospects of winter may not be so daunting, but it is another factor to take into account before deciding where to live.

Do something you've always wanted to do

Lawrence and Katy had always dreamed of moving to the Lake District where they spent most of their holidays and when they had the chance to buy a 17th century coaching inn in Cumbria, they jumped at the chance. Moving from the industrial north, they had no experience in catering or running their own business, but taking a small hotel and 'putting it on the map' was something they'd always wanted to do.

Once their children had settled, Paula and Phillip started an IT business from home. "I just happened to be in the right place at the right time," said Phillip, and within three years it has become a thriving concern. "Lots of people in the country have computers and there's no end to the problems and difficulties they experience, but who do you turn to when things go wrong?"

Alexandra started getting to know people in the community by helping out at a local farmers' market and then progressed to a stall of her own. "I've always loved cooking, so I started off by selling my own jams, preserves and pickles, but it wasn't long before I discovered there was a real need locally for home catering. I now do weddings and suppers and dinner parties for commuting couples who don't have time to cook, and all my ingredients come from fellow stall-holders."

If you feel this is an area you'd like to explore, bear these simple tips in mind when setting up a new farmers' market with like-minded people:

- low stall charges (ie. £5-10 per morning)
- short opening hours (10.00-12.00 noon)
- get certified by the National Association of Farmers' Markets
- have a variety of stall-holders
- if you are starting from scratch, set up the market on a weekday
- keep overheads low and management simple
- be flexible and prepared for change

Be mindful that the natives may be suspicious of anything new, but there's been so much lost within the village communities that any idea might bear fruit if approached from a sensible angle. Take your time and discover what those angles are.

Starting your own business

With so many small businesses closing down in the current economic crisis, there may be all sorts of opportunities for incomers to explore. As one new shopkeeper explained, "The previous couple who ran the shop got it all wrong – they weren't locals, they were unpopular and

110

they didn't understand how to run a village shop. We've only been here two years and we're into profit because we put ourselves out for people."

Village shops tend to be 'open all hours' rather than offering the opportunity to become self-employed and slip into a gentler pace of life. Because these shops (which often include the Post Office) probably provide the only retail outlet in the village, it is necessary to open seven days a week, often remaining open until seven o'clock at night.

Abbie and Sam bought a Welsh long house that had sufficient space for them to utilise two rooms for bed and breakfast guests. As artists they didn't want their home cluttered up with strangers during the day, but the modest income they made through the summer months enabled them to live quite comfortably through the winter.

B&B on working farms is also popular with those who want to explore the countryside. "The first thing that people ask when phoning to book is whether we're a real working farm," said Lynda. "We had to turn our hand to something else because of the 'foot and mouth' crisis a few years back, because even though we didn't loose any of our stock, we couldn't sell it either."

An emphasis on homely rather than hotel, with cosy bedrooms and breakfast served at any time (within reason), may qualify you for approval by Cartwheel, a company set up by those in the farming community to promote farm holidays in the south-west of England. To be accepted on the Cartwheel list of some 200 farms you'll have to be a working farmer who is prepared to offer visitors not just bed and breakfast but also a chance to look (and learn) around the farm. "Flexibility is the key," advises Gina Woodcraft, one of Cartwheel's founders.

On a much larger scale, Liz and David sunk the proceeds from the sale of their home in the Midlands into a collection of dilapidated 19th century commercial buildings in rural mid-Wales. After two years of hard work the properties have been restored as a museum, a guesthouse and a teashop which serves breakfasts and evening meals – they even have room to cater for a 120-delegate conference.

"When we first came to see it," David explained, "we didn't realise we were looking at 50 yards of buildings that were two detached terraces, one behind the other." As well as a comfortable five bedroom house the sale included workshops, a meeting hall, a cart shed, a corn merchant's warehouse, two 17th century tailor's rooms and a former gents' outfitters, closed since 1957 but apparently unchanged since it was opened by the Thomas family around 1805.

In Oxfordshire family enterprise Bramleys Nurseries nurtures not young seedlings but local toddlers. The nursery, which can take over 100 children up to five years old, has recently opened up its state-of-the-art pre-school in one of the units in a series of barn conversions, which also house a phone company, a PR firm, a web designer and a furniture restorer. According to a report in the *Farmers' Weekly* this small development that provides workshop, office and retail space has met the village's need for jobs and childcare while fostering a sense of something new and useful brought into the community.

In the country section of the *Daily Telegraph's* Weekend supplement, a retired businessman talked about the niche he'd found when his daughter opened a delicatessen and experienced problems obtaining supplies of local produce. Although Yorkshire farmers were diversifying, they were only supplying the local corner shops and often lacked the essential marketing skills to sell their products further afield. He identified the opportunity to link rural (and often remote) suppliers of quality produce with retailers who were frustrated by the same difficulty of getting that produce onto their shelves and menus. Within four months around 40 farmers and suppliers had signed up, including producers of meats, poultry, fish, fresh vegetables, dairy products, preserves and chutneys. With the collection and delivery points co-ordinated to minimise unnecessary mileage, they now deliver to shops, hotels and restaurants over a wide area.

Phone the Samaritans!

Isolation is one of the key factors in mental health problems, points out a spokesperson for Mind, the National Association for Mental Health. "It can lead to depression and anxiety if you feel very much alone, without support mechanisms." By interacting with other people we open up our minds to the wider world that involves other people and their viewpoints. If we disconnect ourselves from any social interaction, especially if we've moved to an unfamiliar place where we have no friends or neighbours, we can easily become depressed.

People moving into the country rarely appreciate how difficult it is to make friends, especially if they've left behind a hectic social life. Once the last piece of Portmeirion has been unpacked they look around for a new circle of friends, only to find that the social life is non-existent, and panic sets in. This is particularly true of the wives who are left to moulder in the leafy lanes of the West Country, while the husband is working in the City, or away on a business trip.

The Samaritans receive hundreds of calls from lonely wives who find themselves buried deep in the country and who are desperate for someone to talk to. Sexist comment or not, men rarely appreciate that 'keeping house' is not the sole and life-long ambition of an intelligent woman – even if she does have a kitchen full of top-of-the-range appliances and a new Range Rover on the drive.

At this stage we seriously need to turn to Plan B and refer to the pointers above!

The winter drinks party

Country people are often too busy to socialise during the spring and summer months, but as the seasons change it might be a good idea to organise a winter drinks party to break the ice. Locals will take the occasion quite seriously and it is not too early to send out the invitations 6-8 weeks in advance. These will sit on the mantelpiece for weeks as a reminder that it will be a 7 o'clock start and casual dress.

Needless to say no one turns up until 7.30pm, so don't panic and start hitting the booze thinking that you're going to be ignored. Just brace yourself for the rush and make sure you've somewhere to put the coats where the dog can't nest in them. "The food should be simple, as the grilled squid and chorizo canapés that were a wow in Kensington, will be treated with a great deal of suspicion on Emley Moor," advises Jayne, a Yorkshire farmer's daughter.

Getting it right

- Allow three-quarters to one bottle of wine per person. (In rural areas you are less likely to find an off-licence offering sale or return).
- If you serve red wine, make sure you have a stain remover to hand. (Try Stainaway, a natural enzyme sold by the local vet).

- Hire glasses and order a dozen more than required.

- If you want even numbers, invite more men as they are more likely to drop out.

- Count on a 25% drop-out rate - most at the last minute.

- Make sure the drinks and food tables are centrally placed as a crush of people can make it impossible to get across the room to replenish a guest's glass.

- Offer alternatives to wine, ie. a selection of fruit juices and mineral water.

- Keep the dog out of the 'cloakroom' – even though country people go everywhere with a light dusting of dog hairs on everything.

Journalist Adam Hall observed that, "The English drinks party follows a time-honoured ritual, where sotto voce stiffness slowly breaks into lively chatter and ends in total inebriation. It is hard to believe that the consumption of a cocktail sausage and a fizzy drink can so quickly transform a mumbling troglodyte into a back-slapping buffoon."

By the time your guests leave they will probably have had too much to drink and not enough to eat – and so will you. So do as they do and make sure you have emergency rations waiting in the wings – a large ham and pickle sandwich will do for starters!

Get the occasion right and you will find that the reciprocal invitations will follow; it will be just enough to break the ice without being considered 'pushy,' but remember not to wear your sarong!

THE COUNTRY REALITY

After spending a year in the country we may find ourselves having to define a new set of priorities. Things that seemed so desperately important in urban surroundings don't seem to matter anymore because here no one turns up their nose if mud and straw finds its way into the house. It's not possible to escape mud in the country and in some of the old County family homes the boot room resembles the Somme during the hunting season, even in good weather. You may find that other perspectives have changed and, instead of a monthly subscription to *Country Living*, there will be *Horse & Hound* and/or *The Field* in the magazine rack.

Reality v. illusion

James Douglas writing in *Country Illustrated* observed, "Perhaps the town dwellers, dismayed by the increasing speed at which the quality of urban life is deteriorating, yearn for the consolation of an unreal, dream-fulfilling countryside – a countryside which, alas, never existed, and never will exist, neither here nor anywhere else. Given the state of our towns, it would not be surprising if they did imagine rural England in this light."

And nowhere is this illusion better displayed than when those town dwellers visit friends who have moved to the country. In his book *Out of Your Townie Mind*, Richard Craze (an ex-townie himself) ruefully examines the pitfalls. For example, when you knew your friends in the city, you invariably met up with them for an evening. But the whole point about townie friends, once you have moved to the country, is that they stay for a whole weekend. "They suddenly seem very picky and faddy about food. They insist on seeing all the local tourist attractions, which you've visited every weekend since you moved. They mock you about moving to the sticks, instead of being suitably impressed. They seem bright and fun and young and you realise that living in the country has made you old-fashioned, out of touch and drab." Obviously another book to be read as part of our research exercise!

As the author also goes on to observe, another classic mistake is imagining that because our environment changes, we will automatically change with it. It happens over and over again, where people imagine they will become proficient shooters, gardeners and enjoy tending livestock, only to discover that they have neither the time nor the inclination for gardening, sheep and chickens, or traipsing about over ploughed fields in the depths of winter for a pigeon shoot. Wherever we go we take our lifestyle with us and if lack of time was a major problem in the town, it will still be a major problem in a village. In other words, don't take on six acres of land, a major house renovation or a horse unless you have time for it now!

Legislation

If you thought all those urban rules and regulations were bad enough, spare a thought for the legislation that haunts rural communities – even on private land.

One lunacy was the directive from the European Parliament which voted to toughen the 'Physical Agents (Vibration) Directive' to restrict farmers from driving their own tractors for more than two hours a day. This means that farmers would be unable to plough, sow or harvest their crops as very little can be accomplished in two hours on even a medium-sized farm. Another cunning plan from the same source proposes to ban all two stroke engines which must not be allowed to carry on polluting the atmosphere; this would effectively ban most chainsaws, hedge-trimmers, lawn-mowers and strimmers. This could mean that grass and hedge cutting and tree pruning would have to be carried out by hand using a saw or axe – and the accident rate would soar!

It is only in recent years that the EU managed to pass a directive governing the margins between adjacent arable crops, which should be no more than two metres wide. It never occurred to British representatives that our hedgerows, ditches and uncultivated edges around the fields made it more than twice that width. On one hand, while the government was promoting schemes to pay for hedgerow restoration and wide arable conservation margins, with the other it was signing an agreement that meant that most hedgerows would have to be destroyed for British farmers to comply with EU rules!

One enterprising farmer invited members of the media to a practical demonstration of what the directive meant. He informed them of the content of the directive and then brought in machinery to hack a high and wide 16th century hedge back to a shadow of its former glory, while the media busily filmed and photographed it all. The farmer's action not only saved his remaining hedgerows but also those in the rest of the country.

Another piece of lunacy is the fact that you are no longer allowed to bury any form of livestock on farmland – and this includes a dead lamb, a ferret, a pet cat or a family dog – but you can bury the farmer or his wife! Sooner or later, anyone who is a landowner (even on a very modern scale) will be forced to break a law that has been imposed by someone who has never ventured outside an air-conditioned office in Brussels – even if it's only by giving the family cat a decent burial.

Financial considerations

When Hilary bought her 34 acres in an area of outstanding natural beauty, her only thought was to own the land opposite her house. Without management arable land quickly reverts to scrub and so she has a grazing agreement with a local farmer, who turns out his cows on the pasture. The nature of the agreement means that the land qualifies as a farming business, so Hilary is trading as a farmer.

Julie Butler, author of *Tax Planning for Farm & Land Diversification*, says that there are many landowners "who wake up one day and become farmers whether they like it or not, and sometimes whether they know it or not. Land is not classed as 'agricultural' because it is in an agricultural district but on the use to which it is put. Some uses that may seem agricultural qualify, while others do not. Land let to another farmer for 365 days or more, for example, is not 'agricultural,' but land on which the owner is paid for not growing crops can be."

A spokesman for Knight Frank's country department explains that becoming a farmer allows you to roll over a capital gain you have made in, say, selling a business, if you use the money to buy and develop an agricultural property. The system of reliefs is 'generous but complicated' – as well as free from inheritance tax and the ability to charge up to five years' trading losses against any non-farm income and claim capital gains relief of up to 75% when the land is sold.

Julie Butler, however, sends out this warning: "You can forget buying an attractive cottage in the country, keeping a few sheep or chickens there and claiming all sorts of expenses. Rules to restrict 'hobby farming' date back nearly half a century, but genuine attempts to establish or run an agricultural business are still encouraged by the tax system."

Many schemes for paying farmers for their role as 'carers of the environment' treat them as an extension of DEFRA, with no independent role. In reality, looking after the countryside in the way that 'scientists, naturalists, recreationalists, tourists, sundry pressure-groups, quangos, civil servants, Ministers and the general public' think it should be done is an impossibility. Although the exception is the Environmental Land Management Scheme, which does have the merit of enabling farmers to farm and retain their independence.

'We couldn't live anywhere else'

Regardless of the social and domestic difficulties created by country living, many of those relocating to 'the good life' make the move and settle quite happily. Since Jackie had to finish work due to her pregnancy she's taken more time to look around at her environment and decide that it is a far better place to bring up a child. "The change to a slower pace of life hasn't been easy but I've taken over the paperwork for the farm (which is what I'm good at), which also means that John has more time to concentrate on the practical side of farming. I don't suppose I'll ever make the ideal farmer's wife, but I'm certainly taking more of an interest in what's important to him. I thought I'd return to work after having the baby, but now I'm not so sure."

Reversing the roles, it was Lloyd who had married Lucy, a country-girl, but continued to work in the City. "Having had a bit of a health scare that kept me at home for months on end, I began to really enjoy the healthy environment and fresh air. There was no traffic, no pollution; I could walk out of the house and be aware of the seasons changing. I'm gradually getting back to work but now I mostly work from home. We've kept the flat in London, but we both tend to go up when I have a business meeting, and make an occasion of it.

Annie and Paul took their time in choosing where and how they wanted to live by renting a property for a few months before buying a smallholding. "We liked the location and the people, and we were on the spot when the farm came up for sale. In fact, we'd got on so well with the locals from the pub that one came and banged on the door to tell that the property was coming up for sale. It's been hard work because the place needed a lot doing to it, but we've both got more job satisfaction out of this place than we've ever had in our lives."

Jonie and Michael, who had also spent a long time identifying the kind of country living that would work for them, echoed these sentiments. "Our searches showed us the type of places that wouldn't have been suitable for us in the long term. You can't wear blinkers when making such drastic changes and although some of the locations were spectacular and breathtaking, many of them were just too remote. Just when we were beginning to think we'd never find the ideal place, this little farm came up.....and it's perfect."

When age begins to tell

The inability to integrate into country life is not always the only reason for a move back to town. Paula and Phillip had just reached the stage where they could live the lifestyle they'd always wanted when Phillip had a heart attack and died. "It was doubly hard to cope," says Paula. "We had everything we'd worked for and were happy, and now Phillip's gone. I don't know whether to stay and soldier on, or to move back to town where I'll have more help from the kids. They're getting older and I wonder how long they'll be content to stay here. Do I move now, or wait? I really don't know."

Margaret's daughter was offered a promotion, but it meant her moving to the other end of the country. "I had to decide whether I wanted to stay and only see her on rare occasions, or sell up and move back into a town. In the end, we both decided that I wasn't getting any younger and that it was time to go. I've thoroughly enjoyed the life I've had as part of the village and I'll be leaving lots of friends behind, but I've got to be sensible. As I don't drive, I could find myself making unreasonable, long distance demands on my daughter's time."

Poor public transport is often the clincher. Some areas may have good day time services, while others may only see one bus each week on market days. If one partner suffers from ill-health, or dies, and the other doesn't drive, then there could be all manner of difficulties – especially if the rest of the family live some distance away. Elderly parents living deep in the country will always be a worry to the family, and so pressure might be brought to bear for them to move closer to town.

Children growing up and away at university sometimes find it a long slog to get back to the country for the holidays, often spending most of their time on the phone to friends whose parents also live in some remote beauty spot. It's often hard to accept that they may never come home to live once a career is decided upon, and it may need some careful long term thinking about if you are considering moving a 'tween-age' family to the country.

A richer life

Alexandra and Lewis, however, would not swap their flock of sheep for a king's ransom. "We rarely see friends from our old life any more, simply because the gulf between us kept on widening when we had less and less in common. Our life is here now, and we're all the richer for it. We don't want the razzamatazz of city life and when we had to go back for a big family wedding, we couldn't wait to get back to the farm. We were supposed to stay for a week but we got a friend to phone and say one of the ewes was sick and we had to dash home."

Despite their children integrating well, Allie and Jim found that they had little in common with their farming neighbours and so they started up a social group for others who had moved from the town into the country. "Working from home meant that we never got to meet anyone other than business contacts," said Jim. "In the end Allie put an advert in the local paper for other newcomers to the area who wanted to extend their social life and we've been swamped by calls. So far we've only organised supper parties and theatre trips but there are plenty of other ideas in the pipeline and our lifestyle is now much richer."

Once the neighbours had stopped attempting to snare Stewart for their daughters, he found his own niche with the cricket club and is now secretary. "I can wander into the pub and have a drink or supper with some of the other members, and often get invited to family parties. The cricket club had quite a healthy social life of its own, so there's no shortage of company – and I've just met a really lovely lady who's just moved into the village."

Roger and Maeve find that they have few problems living in a village, despite Roger's frequent trips to the hospital for suspected diabetes. "Even the hospital staff have more time for you and you can't get away from the kindness. Even if we had to get rid of the car we can still get about because we belong to so many different things that we would never be without transport. We'd never go back to town."

When dreams turn to ashes

But what happens when things don't work out as planned and life in a rural idyll loses its allure? Many are finding that the muddy fields and misty mornings can't compensate for the lack of friends and the bright lights. "The fact is, this place doesn't suit us any more. We're bored and it's time to go back," admitted Trish. "We were fine for the first couple of years when it was all new, but if we're really honest we are fish out of water and don't know quite what we're doing here."

Despite buying a 17th century country house with all the right ingredients for a dream home, within three years Jennifer and Geoff were ready to move back to town. They hated the country and they didn't fit in. "There were some weeks when I didn't really talk to anyone at all, and I felt very isolated," explained Jennifer. "There wasn't anyone I could call on for a coffee and a chat and, being perfectly truthful, we found the whole farming and hunting scene a complete turn-off."

Martin and Chris also found that the isolation from their own circle of friends was beginning to create a rift in their relationship. "Being a gay couple in a rural community isn't easy," Martin confessed. "We thought we'd brazen it out and they'd come round in time, but this hasn't happened. Country folk don't embrace change and although everyone is perfectly civil, we've not made any real friends. We've had a good offer for the restaurant and so I think it's time we moved on before we kiss each other goodbye. It has put quite a strain on our relationship."

Back to town

City dwellers fed up with stories of the utopian lifestyle of friends who move to the countryside will be comforted by the findings of a recent survey. A move to the countryside to work from home often goes wrong, according to a survey commissioned by Sainsbury's Bank. Researchers found that a quarter of the people who sold their city homes and moved to the country admitted that their lives were more difficult and frustrating and that the lack of stimulation had led to depression, headaches and fatigue.

In fact, for the first time in years as many people are now moving from the country to the city as vice-versa because newcomers find they cannot cope with what they see as isolation and boredom. This often becomes a problem when the children get older. Small children grow and flourish in a rural environment, but once they reach their teens with the prospect of university and/or a new career looming large, frustration and boredom can take its toll.

This is why it may be more practical to look at properties on the edge of a market town or coastal area, since this will run less risk of creating divisions within the family in years to come. "Unless children have grown up in a rural community, there is little to keep them there once they hit puberty," remarked Chris. "We have some serious discussions coming up about whether we move nearer to town or not once the boys finish school, because there's nothing here for them career-wise. Both children have a good distance to travel every day to school, and it means that in the evenings and at weekends they are a long way from their friends. As a result they get bored and we are all constantly bickering about the most trivial of things. With hindsight I wish we lived nearer town, but it's something you don't think about when you first talk about moving to the country."

A few final words of caution

123

Country living, like most things in life, will not suit everyone. Choosing to move to an expensive property in a rural village in the heart of a farming community will not guarantee acceptance. Gabrielle and her husband moved back to the country after an enforced period in town and bought their house at a give-away price from a family who couldn't wait to get out. "The wife hated it so much that she couldn't keep quiet about how snobby the neighbours were and how they wouldn't talk to her, but within weeks we'd been invited to all sorts of social events. In truth, we are country people, and although not from this area we know how to behave and integrate into village life."

Don and Linda moved from London to an idyllic but remote country house. A few months down the line and Linda was driven to distraction by the day-to-day loneliness. A move back to London was tempting, but in the end they gambled on another move closer to a small town and like-minded neighbours. Property was more expensive but it was a trade-off they were only too willing to make. They sensibly realised that choosing the right place to live was not just about bricks and mortar because finding an ideal home is determined just as much by how we want to live our lives.

"Too many people make the mistake of thinking that by buying that dream house they will be able to slot into the rural idyll overnight. A distance of just a few miles can make all the difference as to whether the move is going to work or not," advised Linda, who is now happily settled in her new home.

Signposts For Country Living may not paint the colourful pictures of the glossy magazines, but it is honest about the difficulties and problems that many people have encountered when they exchange the city suit for a waxed jacket. These experiences, however, have not been without their humour and most of those who have told stories about themselves are still there tending the sheep, running the shops and market stalls, riding to hounds or entering the family lurcher for a race at the local Game Fair. They stay because they have made the transition from town to country and become valued members of their community.

They are now living their dream.....and so is the dog.

Further Reading

Any Fool's Country Life by James Robertson
The Farmer Wants A Wife by Maeve Haran
Food For Free by Richard Mabey
Out Of Your Townie Mind by Richard Craze

Magazines

Home Famer
Smallholder
Country Smallholding

Websites

www.homefarmer.co.uk
www.thedownshifter.co.uk
www.acountrylife.co.uk
www.rivercottage.net
www.selfsufficientish.com

THE DOWNSHIFTER'S JOKE BOOK

By

LES ELLIS

When you think about it, anyone wanting to quit a comfortable, well-paid job with a pension and an expense account to go and work for nothing, knee deep in something, is comical and Les's cartoons certainly help us to see the funny side of most things that smallholders, downshifters and good lifers seem to get up to.

This book is guaranteed to bring a laugh at the turn of each and every page as Les's sharp, inspired drawings and slyly topical captions take a gentle but loving dig at downshifters, townies and rural living and a rather less kind dig at red tape, politicians and anybody else who regularly gets on our wick.

Les began drawing seriously at school and, although he was never really interested in painting any of the 'still life stuff,' he often drew wickedly funny caricatures of the teaching staff for the amusement of his friends, if not the staff itself.

On growing up he got a 'proper' job in an office, but quit in a temporary moment of sanity to set up a gardening business with his wife. He has not looked back since, and now, 4 years later, his quality of life (unlike his bank account) is much improved.

Les decided to get back to what he really loved – cartoons and his regular feature in Home Farmer has become a sure hit with the readers, to the point that he is now being asked for the originals (and not only as evidence by the plaintiffs' solicitors).

ISBN 9781904871835
Published by The Good Life Press Ltd.

ANY FOOL CAN BE A.....
PIG FARMER

By

JAMES ROBERTSON

This, the first of James Robertson's sagas about agriculture and country life, demonstrates that the young and inexperienced Robertson was even move prone to disaster than the older and still inexperienced Robertson. His pigs bit him, gave him lice, crawled up to his bed and indicated that man is not necessarily the dominant species.

How do you communicate the facts of life to an innocent young boar, persuade a sow not to eat her young, survive an investigation by the Inland Revenue and stay out of jail when your newly insured barn goes up in smoke?

Set amid the picturesque slag heaps of the North Wales borders, Any Fool Can Be a..... Pig Farmer shows the other side of the rural idyll. It is painful, real and very funny.

ISBN 9781904871712

Published by The Good Life Press Ltd.

The Good Life Press Ltd.
The Old Pigsties
Clifton Fields
Lytham Road
Preston PR4 0XG
01772 633444

The Good Life Press Ltd. publishes a wide range of titles for the smallholder, 'goodlifer' and farmer. We also publish **Home Farmer,** the monthly magazine for anyone who wants to grab a slice of the good life - whether they live in the country or the city. Other titles of interest include:

A Guide to Traditional Pig Keeping by Carol Harris
An Introduction to Keeping Cattle by Peter King
An Introduction to Keeping Sheep by J. Upton/D. Soden
Any Fool Can Be a.....Dairy Farmer by James Robertson
Any Fool Can Be a.....Pig Farmer by James Robertson
Any Fool Can Be a..... Middle Aged Downshifter by Mike Woolnough
Build It! by Joe Jacobs
Build It!....With Pallets by Joe Jacobs
Craft Cider Making by Andrew Lea
Flowerpot Farming by Jayne Neville
Making Country Wines, Ales and Cordials by Brian Tucker
Making Jams and Preserves by Diana Sutton
No Time to Grow? by Tim Wootton
Precycle! by Paul Peacock
Raising Chickens for Eggs and Meat by Mike Woolnough
Raising Goats by Felicity Stockwell
Showing Sheep by Sue Kendrick
The Bread and Butter Book by Diana Sutton
The Cheese Making Book by Paul Peacock
The Frugal Life by Piper Terrett
The Medicine Garden by Rachel Corby
The Pocket Guide to Wild Food by Paul Peacock
The Polytunnel Companion by Jayne Neville
The Sausage Book by Paul Peacock
The Secret Life of Cows by Rosamund Young
The Sheep Book for Smallholders by Tim Tyne
The Smallholder's Guide to Animal Ailments Ed. Russell Lyons
The Smoking and Curing Book by Paul Peacock
Worms and Wormeries by Mike Woolnough

www.goodlifepress.co.uk
www.homefarmer.co.uk